CW00428314

New
Scottish Poetry

Published by Heinemann Educational Publishers
Halley Court, Jordan Hill, Oxford OX2 8EJ
A division of Reed Educational and Professional Publishing Ltd

OXFORD MELBOURNE AUCKLAND
JOHANNESBURG BLANTYRE GABORONE
IBADAN PORTSMOUTH (NH)USA CHICAGO

04 03 02 01
10 9 8 7 6 5 4 3 2 1

ISBN 0 435 15098 7

ACKNOWLEDGEMENTS
The publishers gratefully acknowledge the following for permission to reproduce
copyright material. Every effort has been made to trace copyright holders, but in
some cases this has proved impossible. The publishers would be happy to hear
from any copyright holder that has not been acknowledged.

'Divorce' from *Three Has Gone* by Jackie Kay, published by Blackie. Copyright ©
1994 by Jackie Kay; reprinted by permission of Peters, Fraser & Dunlop Group on
behalf of Jackie Kay. 'Whistle Down the Wind', 'Bed', 'Pride', and 'False Memory'
from *Off Colour*, published by Bloodaxe Books, 1998; reprinted with permission
of Bloodaxe Books Ltd. 'Dressing Up', 'He Told Us He Wanted a Black Coffin',
and 'I try my absolute best' from *Adoption Papers* by Jackie Kay, published by
Bloodaxe Books, 1991; reprinted with permission of Bloodaxe Books Ltd. 'The
Queen of Sheba', 'Wee Baby' and 'Wee Wifey' from *The Queen of Sheba* by
Kathleen Jamie, published by Bloodaxe Books, 1994; reprinted with permission
of Bloodaxe Books Ltd. 'Thaw', 'Bairnsang', 'Crossing the Loch' and 'The Soldier'
from *Jizzen* by Kathleen Jamie, published by Picador, 1999; reprinted with
permission of Macmillan Publishers Ltd. 'The Pheasant Lesson', 'Roadkill',
'Corbandie' and 'The Ballad of Technofear' by W.N. Herbert, from *Cabaret
McGonagall*, published by Bloodaxe Books, 1996; reprinted with permission of
Bloodaxe Books Ltd. 'Grey Thrums' from *The Laurelude* by W.N. Herbert,
published by Bloodaxe Books, 1998; reprinted with permission of Bloodaxe
Books Ltd. 'Valentine', 'Small Female Skull', 'Away and See' and 'The Grammar

of Light' from *Mean Time* by Carol Ann Duffy, published by Anvil Press Poetry, 1993; reprinted with permission of Anvil Press Poetry Ltd. 'A Healthy Meal' from *Standing Female Nude* by Carol Ann Duffy, published by Anvil Press Poetry, 1985; reprinted with permission of Anvil Press Poetry Ltd. 'Mrs Sisyphus', 'Mrs Icarus' and 'Circe' from *The World's Wife* by Carol Ann Duffy, published by Picador, 1999; reprinted with permission of Macmillan Publishers Ltd. 'Visiting my Grandfather', 'Advent in Co. Fermanagh', 'Retreat', 'Fireworks' and 'The Spanish Dancer' from *A Painted Field* by Robin Robertson, published by Picador, 1997; reprinted with permission of Macmillan Publishers Ltd. 'Fishing Boats and Ferries', 'Snow and Salt', 'Young Chinese and Scottish', 'The Bar Flea', and 'Am Bogha-frois Briste/The Broken Rainbow' from *Love and Zen in the Outer Hebrides* by Kevin MacNeil, published by Canongate Books Ltd, 1998; reprinted with permission of Canongate Books Ltd. 'An dèidh an Tòrraidh/After the Funeral', ''S e mo ghaol a' ghrian san adhar/My love is the sun in the sky', 'Oran sa Gheamhradh/Song in Winter' and 'Dha mo Naoidhean air Ur-bhreith/To my New-born Child' from *Lightness and Other Poems* by Meg Bateman, published by Polygon, 1997; reprinted with permission of Edinburgh University Press. 'Men from the Boys', 'The Flautist', 'Pathetic Fallacy', 'Patagonia' and 'Double Take' from *Slattern* by Kate Clanchy, published by Chatto & Windus, 1996; used by permission of The Random House Group Ltd. 'War Poetry' and 'Heliograph' from *Samarkand* by Kate Clanchy, published by Picador, 1999; reprinted with permission of Macmillan Publishers Ltd. 'The Freedom', 'Anorexia', 'Unemployed', 'Night Shift', 'The Pictures' and 'Ponytail' from *Coming Out With It* by Angela McSeveney, published by Polygon, 1992; reprinted with permission of Edinburgh University Press. 'Going Back to Chapelton', 'Autumn in the Graveyard', 'Untitled Love Poem', 'Colonizers', 'Jesus Speaks to the Church at Eastertime', 'Ophelia' and 'At Plath's Grave' from *Ophelia and Other Poems* by Elizabeth Burns, published by Polygon, 1991; reprinted with permission of Edinburgh University Press. 'Brother' and 'Exile's Return' from *The Hoop* by John Burnside, published by Carcanet Press; reprinted with permission of Carcanet Press Ltd. 'Otherlife', 'The Men's Harbour' and 'Geese' from *The Asylum Dance* by John Burnside, published by Jonathan Cape, 2000; used by permission of The Random House Group Ltd. 'Oriental Sunset', 'No Name Woman', 'Lesson', 'A Beginning', 'Mr Punch, The Ubiquitous Farçeur', 'Four Canadian Shorts', 'Fantasy' and 'Tattoo' from *Madame Doubtfire's Dilemma* by Dilys Rose; reprinted with the kind permission of the author. 'Heliographer', 'Close', 'Wind-Tunnel' and 'Next to Nothing', from *Nil Nil* by Don Paterson, '11:00: Baldovan' from *God's Gift to Women* (1997) by Don Paterson, 'The Visit' and 'The Work' from *The Eyes* (1999) by Don Paterson, all published by Faber and Faber Ltd; reprinted with permission of Faber and Faber Ltd.

Designed and produced by 320 Design

Printed and bound in Great Britain

CONTENTS

INTRODUCTION

The poems in *New Scottish Poetry* have been selected for enjoyment and study by young adults in schools and colleges. More specifically, within the English and Communication Arrangements for Higher Still, they offer opportunities to develop the students' skills in reading and responding to poetry which culminate in the Critical Essay and Textual Analysis.

The word 'New' in the title guarantees that nearly all the poems have been published for the first time in book form in the 1990s. The poets are in their twenties, thirties and forties – a new generation of vigorous Scottish writers who have galloped away with many of poetry's most prestigious prizes. And the issues they address are very much those of twenty-first century Scotland.

In this selection we have been careful to include poems with a range of levels of difficulty. Able students at Higher Level will be suitably challenged by poets such as Robin Robertson, Carol Ann Duffy or Don Paterson; students at Intermediate 1 and Access 3 will find they can read and respond to Jackie Kay and Angela McSeveney. But most of the poets write poems of varying difficulty: Jackie Kay's 'Divorce', for example, is written for young people and immediately accessible to all. However, her poem 'Pride' will require the experience and skill of Higher students; while students at Intermediate levels may take better to 'Whistle Down the Wind'. We believe teachers will prefer to judge for themselves the appropriateness of the poems for the varied abilities of their own students.

The poems are written in English, Scots or Gaelic. Those in Scots are glossed and the Gaelic poems are accompanied by the poets' own translations, the majority of which constitute poems in their own right. The poems in Scots are in different dialects – W.N. Herbert, for example, writing in distinctive Dundonian (the Analysis and Evaluation section in **Activities** offers help with this – see page 107).

A significant number of poets write in two languages and there are enough poems from each poet for students to pursue into Specialist Study. The poems offer opportunities in Specialist Study of both Language and Literature. The poems by W.N. Herbert or Kevin MacNeil, for example, offer excellent starting points for *personal or local* Specialist Language Study. As there is an emphasis on *poems related by theme or style* in Specialist Literature Study, there is a thematic listing of the poems (on page 136).

Mindful of the need to provide an integrated curriculum in English and Communication, the **Activities** section at the back provides not just questions for the poems (in both the Understanding and the Analysis and Evaluation sections) but also suggestions on how the issues in the poems can be further explored through Group Discussion, Individual Presentation and Creative Writing activities.

It is anticipated that at Intermediate and Access levels students will encounter poetry initially in teacher-led discussion. The Arrangements document advises us to identify first *the key elements and central concerns of the text*; and from there to uncover *ways in which aspects of structure, style and language contribute to the meaning, effect or impact of the text*. Accordingly, in the Understanding section of the **Activities**, we have tried to find a key question to prise open the basic situation/idea/meaning/intention of the poem.

Accepting again the advice of the Arrangements document to proceed by *consulting and comparing a number of texts*, this question frequently asks the reader to compare or contrast two or three poems by the same writer; but the question can readily be modified to address just one poem. The same approach is used in the Analysis and Evaluation section, where we have included questions intended to reveal the key techniques of the same poem(s). At Intermediate and Access levels, however, these questions will need to be split into easier steps and asked in simpler terms through teacher-led discussion.

In the **Activities** section the questions are designed to allow students at Higher level to work independently of the teacher. In line with the emphasis in the Performance Criteria for Literary Study on the use of critical terminology, the questions deliberately set out to enhance the students' critical vocabulary. However, since students at Higher level vary in ability, teachers will find that, for some, prior discussion of the terminology will be helpful. While it is not the purpose of this anthology to offer opportunities for unseen textual analysis, the Critical Essay and Textual Analysis share performance criteria and the Understanding and the Analysis and Evaluation sections are designed to help students develop skills essential for both.

At the end of the Analysis and Evaluation section for each poet we have included a question of the kind students will encounter in the Critical Essay. The question asks them to write about one or more of the poems by the poet they have been studying and will use the format found in the external examination of the Critical Essay. As required in the Performance Criteria, the essay will also incorporate the dimension of student engagement with the text in varying degrees.

The English and Communications Arrangements document stresses the importance of deriving support for group discussion, individual presentation and writing from the reading programme. In the **Activities** section, therefore, in the section on Group Discussion and Individual Presentation, there are suggestions that draw upon the significant ideas/issues in the poems. Opportunities for group discussion on the poems will already have arisen from the Understanding and the Analysis and Evaluation sections. However, the ideas and issues being explored through talk in the Group Discussion and Individual Presentation section can be extended, as the Arrangements recommend, into *Reflective, Persuasive, or Report Writing*. There are examples of these where appropriate.

Finally in the **Activities** section, under each poet, there is a suggestion for creative writing arising from the poems. The Arrangements document advocates support for students' own creative writing through the use of the models/styles/voices/ideas found in the study of literature. The voices, structures and styles of these younger Scottish poets are as vigorous as they are various. They can usefully be copied, in story and drama as well as poetry, as a starting point for students' creative writing, and teachers will no doubt expand on the suggestions we have had room to offer.

A.G., G.L., Glasgow, February 2001

JACKIE KAY

Whistle Down the Wind

My brother has his fingers,
dirt under the over-long nails,
on the tin whistle
he doesn't know how to play.
Its sharp insolent notes
speak for him
since he is an adolescent
and adolescents don't talk or listen.

I am not yet one of those, but can't
imagine me not-talking, but then
I am, according to my brother,
Miss Goody Two Shoes.

Suddenly, he rises up from the armchair
where he has been sitting,
screaming out the spiteful folksongs
of his own making;
takes his whistle
and, for no good reason, whacks
me straight across the face.

My mother is up on her feet,
pushing him and he is falling backwards
as my mother screams *her face you've got her face.*
I've got no face.
My brother has got my face in his hands,
shaking it back and forth.

My face is rubber; sly as a mask.
He's in trouble this time.
Big trouble. The sting of tin is sweet after all.
Big big trouble. I feel myself laugh under my ice jaw.
My two shoes get gooder and gooder.

But he never was.
Big Trouble never arrived on its noble horse
with its long whip to save me.

Oh whistle and I'll come tae you my lass.

Dressing Up

(*for Toby*)

My family's all so squalid
I'm trying to put it behind
me – real typical working class
Scottish: Da beats Ma drinks it off.
I couldn't stomach it, banging

doors, turning ma music up top
blast. I told ma ma years ago. She'd
rather I murdered somebody than
that. She wasn't joking either.
Nobody gets hurt, it's not for

the image even I'm just dead
childish. Mascara I like, rouge,
putting it on after powder.
I love wearing lots of layers.
Ma ma always dresses boring

No frills. See at Christmas I had
on black stockings Santa would kill
for and even Quentin Crisp would
look drab beside my beautiful
feather boa – bright fucking red.

Ma ma didn't touch her turkey
Finally she said What did I do
I know what they call you, transvite.
You look a bloody mess you do.
She had a black eye, a navy dress.

Divorce

I did not promise
to stay with you till death us do part, or
anything like that,
so part I must, and quickly. There are things
I cannot suffer
any longer: Mother, you have never, ever, said
a kind word
or a thank you for all the tedious chores I have done;
Father, your breath
smells like a camel's and gives me the hump;
all you ever say is:
'Are you off in the cream puff, Lady Muck?'
In this day and age?
I would be better off in an orphanage.

I want a divorce.
There are parents in the world whose faces turn
up to the light
who speak in the soft murmur of rivers
and never shout.
There are parents who stroke their children's cheeks
in the dead night
and sing in the colourful voices of rainbows,
red to blue.
These parents are not you. I never chose you.
You are rough and wild,
I don't want to be your child. All you do is shout
and that's not right.
I will file for divorce in the morning at first light.

Bed

She is that guid tae me so she is
an Am a burden tae her, I know Am ur.
Stuck here in this big blastit bed
year in, year oot, ony saint wuid complain.

There's things she has tae dae fir me
A' wish she didnae huv tae dae.
Am her wean* noo, wey ma great tent o' nappy,
an champed egg in a cup, an mashed tattie.

Aw the treats A' used tae gie her,
she's gieing me. A' dinny ken whit happened.
We dinny talk any mair. Whether it's jist
the blethers ha been plucked oot o' us

an Am here like some skinny chicken,
ma skin aw bubbles and dots and spots,
loose flap noo (an yet as a young wuman
A' took pride in ma guid smooth skin.)

Aw A' dae is sit an look oot this windae.
A've seen hale generations graw up
an simmer doon fray this same windae –
that's no seen a lick o' paint fir donkeys.

The Kerrs have disappeared, but the last
Campbells ur still here so Am telt –
tho' hauf the time A' dinny believe her:
A've no seen ony Campbell in a lang time.

My dochter* says 'Awright mother?'
haunds me a thin broth or puried neep
an A say 'Aye fine,' an canny help
the great heaving sigh that comes oot

wean: a child
dochter: daughter

my auld loose lips, nor ma crabbit tut,
nor ma froon when A' pu' ma cardie tight
aroon ma shooders fir the night drawin in.
Am jist biding time so am ur.

Time is whit A' hauld between
the soft bits o' ma thumbs,
the skeleton underneath ma night goon;
aw the while the glaring selfish moon

lights up this drab wee prison.
A'll be gone and how wull she feel?
No that Am saying A' want her guilty.
No that Am saying Am no grateful.

He Told Us He Wanted a Black Coffin

(*for Margaret McAllister*)

I phoned up the funeral director,
he said it would cost us a fortune
so we bought an ordinary pine one
painted it black matt like his furniture.
It looked smashing. He went out
like Charles Rennie Mackintosh –
a single bunch of white lilies on top.
None but Derek's flowers.

These past few days I can't stop thinking
how I wanted to take the abscess out
of his five year old mouth and put it in mine;
I wanted to fall off that wall in Greig Street;
the day I swore at Mrs Calder
for calling my son a poof in front of hers.
I always knew from when he was thirteen
and he cried when Gavin moved to Aberdeen.

No morphine no morphine no morphine
I want to be alive when I'm alive
dead when I'm dead know what I mean.
No first aid box to fetch,
No oil of cloves, no germolene
nothing, nothing – his hand in mine
his thumb tap tapping my palm
me saying you're all right son.

Everything is all messed up.
The boy careening down the hill in the park
his sledge a huge pair of wings, scarf flying.
The man in my kitchen laughing at my bad jokes
(who'll laugh now?) The man in the hospital bed
the size of the boy; his face a person from Belsen.
The song he sang at the school concert
(what was it?) It doesn't seem that long ago.

I try my absolute best

I give my kids pure apple juice
(no sugar less acid than orange)
buy my baby soya milk formula
now she's off the breast
(non dairy, no cholesterol, good
for their little hearts – apparently
their arteries can harden before five
even). Water from the purifier.
Perrier if I'm feeling flush,
(they can always pretend it's lemonade).
Carob coated date bars. Cherry or banana.
And there's a shop down the street
that is selling organic vegetables
(no sprays, no chemicals).
Only to find the bloody English apples
are being sprayed with alar and are
carcinogenic; the soya beans are cooked

in aluminium pots which gives off deposits
in the brain; the cartridge in the purifier
collects things (like knickers if they're not changed).
Perrier's got Benzene in it which gives rats
cancer. Though I personally don't know any rat
that drinks Perrier, do you? And them
so-called Health Food Bars contain more sugar
than the average Mars Bar. What's the use
in calling anything organic when
the bloody soil's chock-a-block with lead?

I try my absolute best
drink decaff coffee to pipe me down
instead of hype me up only to find
out from my eldest daughter
that what they put the beans through
is worse for you than an ordinary Nescafé.

I'm back on Valium.
My kids are stuffing Monster Munch
and Mars Bars down them.
My youngest son even ate a hamburger yesterday.
It's driving me crazy.
I says it's your pocket money,
Do what you want with it.

Pride

When I looked up, the black man was there,
staring into my face,
as if he had always been there,
as if he and I went a long way back.
He looked into the dark pool of my eyes
as the train slid out of Euston.
For a long time this went on
the stranger and I looking at each other,
a look that was like something being given
from one to the other.

My whole childhood, I'm quite sure,
passed before him, the worst things
I've ever done, the biggest lies I've ever told.
And he was a little boy on a red dust road.
He stared into the dark depth of me,
and then he spoke:
'Ibo,' he said. 'Ibo, definitely.'
Our train rushed through the dark.
'You are an Ibo!' he said, thumping the table.
My coffee jumped and spilled.
Several sleeping people woke.
The night train boasted and whistled
through the English countryside,
past unwritten stops in the blackness.

'That nose is an Ibo nose.
Those teeth are Ibo teeth,' the stranger said,
his voice getting louder and louder.
I had no doubt, from the way he said it,
that Ibo noses are the best noses in the world,
that Ibo teeth are perfect pearls.
People were walking down the trembling aisle
to come and look
as the night rain babbled against the window.
There was a moment when
my whole face changed into a map,
and the stranger on the train
located even the name
of my village in Nigeria
in the lower part of my jaw.

I told him what I'd heard was my father's name.
Okafor. He told me what it meant,
something stunning,
something so apt and astonishing.
Tell me, I asked the black man on the train
who was himself transforming,
at roughly the same speed as the train,
and could have been

at any stop, my brother, my father as a young man,
or any member of my large clan,
Tell me about the Ibos.

His face had a look
I've seen on a MacLachlan, a MacDonnell, a MacLeod,
the most startling thing, pride,
a quality of being certain.
Now that I know you are an Ibo, we will eat.
He produced a spicy meat patty,
ripping it into two.
Tell me about the Ibos.
'The Ibos are small in stature
Not tall like the Yoruba or Hausa.
The Ibos are clever, reliable,
dependable, faithful, true.
The Ibos should be running Nigeria.
There would be none of this corruption.'

And what, I asked, are the Ibos' faults?
I smiled my newly acquired Ibo smile,
flashed my gleaming Ibo teeth.
The train grabbed at a bend,
'Faults? No faults. Not a single one.'

'If you went back,' he said brightening,
'The whole village would come out for you.
Massive celebrations. Definitely.
Definitely,' he opened his arms wide.
'The eldest grandchild – fantastic welcome.
If the grandparents are alive.'

I saw myself arriving
the hot dust, the red road,
the trees heavy with other fruits,
the bright things, the flowers.
I saw myself watching
the old people dance towards me
dressed up for me in happy prints.

And I found my feet.
I started to dance.
I danced a dance I never knew I knew.
Words and sounds fell out of my mouth like seeds.
I astonished myself.
My grandmother was like me exactly, only darker.

When I looked up, the black man had gone.
Only my own face startled me in the dark train window.

False Memory

It came to her when she was out
walking and it stopped her dead.
She must have stood there
for a lifetime like a tree
rooted to the spot,
her thin arms jabbing the wind.

Don't tell me it is not true.
His hair is falling over my face.
I can still see him
coming through the crack of light
at the bottom of my room,
splitting me open like a nut.

For a long time she blotted him out.
She didn't know why her mouth spluttered
wet, nervous laughter
after each time she saw him or why
she hid him tucked up in the hem of her skirt
or why she scrubbed the back of her neck.

I would love him to be false,
no flesh or blood, no shadow or beard,
no looming booming presence in a room,
to be all lies, fake, fiction, sham.
A bit of her would rather not remember;
but when I did the memory was a flood

pouring itself out, murky and green
all the riverbanks swollen, gushing
incidents from my life, his face, my face
the dark all lit up
and suddenly my small house
was floating on the water.

I saw myself, nine years old,
shipwrecked, soaked, floating down
the river with the lovely name,
the name I can't speak,
without filling again, as if the
river was my childhood,

as if I could say I was
down by the river with the lovely name,
and none of it happened;
it didn't happen because I was busy.
I was busy fishing for tadpoles or trout
or watching dragonflies
or looking for interesting debris –
a new word I had just learnt and loved to use.

Life is full of debris
I would say to my girlfriends
and none of it would have happened.
But one night it did
And then it happened again.
And then it happened again.

The focus blurred, blunt edges,
a family album, grins and grimaces.
The dark developing night.
Now I can peel back the wet
pages, and let her out,
carefully. I won't damage her head.

KATHLEEN JAMIE

The Queen of Sheba

Scotland, you have invoked her name
just once too often
in your Presbyterian living rooms.
She's heard, yea
even unto heathenish Arabia
your vixen's bark of poverty, come down
the family like a lang neb, a thrawn streak*,
a wally dug* you never liked
but can't get shot of.

She's had enough. She's come.
Whit, tae this dump? Yes!
She rides first camel
of a swaying caravan
from her desert sands
to the peat and bracken
of the Pentland hills
across the fit-ba pitch
to the thin mirage
of the swings and chute; scattered with glass.

Breathe that steamy musk
on the Curriehill Road, not mutton-shanks
boiled for broth, nor the chlorine stink
of the swimming pool where skinny girls
accuse each other of verrucas.
In her bathhouses women bear

thrawn streak: stubborn or awkward strain in someone's
    character
wally dug: ornamental china dog

warm pot-bellied terracotta pitchers
on their laughing hips.
All that she desires, whatever she asks
She will make the bottled dreams
of your wee lasses
look like *sweeties*.

Spangles scarcely cover
her gorgeous breasts, hanging gardens
jewels, frankincense; more voluptuous
even than Vi-next-door, whose
high-heeled slippers
keeked from dressing gowns
like little hooves, wee tails
of pink fur stuffed in the cleavage of her toes;
more audatious even than Currie Liz
who led the gala floats
through the Wimpey scheme
in a ruby-red Lotus Elan
before the Boys' Brigade band
and the Brownies' borrowed coal-truck;
hair piled like candy-floss;
who lifted like hands from the neat wheel
to tinkle her fingers
at her tricks
    among the Masons and the elders and the police.

The cool black skin
of the Bible couldn't hold her,
nor the atlas green
on the kitchen table,
you stuck with thumbs
and split to fruity hemispheres –
yellow Yemen, Red Sea, *Ethiopia*. Stick in
with the homework and you'll be
cliver like yer faither.
but no too cliver,
no *above yersel*.

See her lead those great soft camels
widdershins round the kirk-yaird,
smiling
as she eats
avocados with apostle spoons
she'll teach us how. But first

she wants to strip the willow
she desires the keys
        to the National Library
she is beckoning
        the lasses
        in the awestruck crowd ...

Yes, we'd like to
        clap the camels,
to smell the spice,
admire her hairy legs and
bonny wicked smile, we want to take
PhDs in Persian, be vice
to her president: we want
to help her
        ask some Difficult Questions

she's shouting for our wisest man
to test her mettle:

        Scour Scotland for a Solomon!

Sure enough: from the back of the crowd
someone growls:
                whae do you think y'ur?

and a thousand laughing girls and she
draw our hot breath
        and shout:

THE QUEEN OF SHEBA!

Wee Baby

In a dark and private place –
                     your handbag
she knits herself existence.
She sums and divides herself
from half-forgotten phone numbers.

She has slavered on the future
pages of your diary
to make
    a papier-mâché baby
she rubs herself with lipstick,

renders herself visible,
because she only just exists, like a stamp hinge.

She sticks. She dangles from her fathers.
She turns little fishy tricks
in your wine glass: you swallow,
now:
    open your mouth and who cries out?

Wee Baby's come to work:
she is tucked up in the in-tray.
Wee Baby's in the kitchen:
she is cradled in the sieve of all potential.

She blows about the desert in a sand-pram,
O traveller. And driver –
who flashes so indignant
on the outside lane?

She's on the town tonight, she's giving her first smile,
she's playing with her toes
on a high and lonely bar-stool.
You know you're thirty, and she loves you.

The kingdom of Wee Baby is within.
She curls her fists and holds tight.

Wee Wifey

I have a demon and her name is
                    WEE WIFEY
I caught her in a demon trap – the household of my skull
I pinched her by the heel throughout her wily transformations
until
        she confessed
                    her name indeed to be WEE WIFEY
and she was out to do me ill.

So I made great gestures like Jehovah: dividing
land from sea, sea from sky,
                    my own self from WEE WIFEY
(*There*, she says, *that's tidy!*)

Now I watch her like a dolly
keep an eye,
            and mourn her:
For she and I are angry/cry
                    because we love each other dearly.

It's sad to note
            that without
                    WEE WIFEY
I shall live long and lonely as a tossing cork.

Thaw

When we brought you home in a taxi
through the steel-grey thaw
after the coldest week in memory
– even the river sealed itself –
it was I, hardly breathing,
who came through the passage to our yard
welcoming our simplest things:
a chopping block, the frost-
split lintels; and though it meant a journey
through darkening snow,
arms laden with you in a blanket,
I had to walk to the top of the garden,
to touch, in a complicit
homage of equals, the spiral
trunks of our plum trees, the moss,
the robin's roost in the holly.
Leaning back on the railway wall,
I tried to remember;
but even my footprints were being erased
and the rising stars of Orion
denied what I knew: that as we were
hurled on a trolley through swing doors to theatre
they'd been there, aligned on the ceiling,
    ablaze with concern
for that difficult giving,
before we were two, from my one.

Bairnsang

Wee toshie man,
   gean tree and rowan
gif ye could staun,
yer feet wad lichtsome tread
granite an saun,
but ye cannae yet staun
sae maun courie tae ma airm
an greetna, girna, Gretna Green

Peedie wee lad
   saumon, siller haddie
gin ye could rin
ye'd rin richt easy-strang
ower causey* an carse*,
but ye cannae yet rin
sae maun jist courie in
and fashna, fashna, Macrahanish Sand

Bonny wee boy
   peeswheep an whaup
gin ye could sing, yer sang
wad be caller
as a lauchin mountain burn
but ye cannae yet sing
sae maun courie tae ma hert
an grieve nat at aa, Ainster an Crail

My ain tottie bairn
   sternie* an lift*
gin ye could daunce, yer daunce
wad be that o life itsel,
but ye cannae yet daunce
sae maun courie in my erms
and sleep, saftly sleep, Unst and Yell

causey: street   *sternie:* star
carse: field   *lift:* sky

Crossing the Loch

Remember how we rowed toward the cottage
on the sickle-shaped bay,
that one night after the pub
loosed us through its swinging doors
and we pushed across the shingle
till water lipped the sides
as though the loch mouthed 'boat'?

I forget who rowed. Our jokes hushed.
The oars' splash, creak, and the spill
of the loch reached long into the night.
Out in the race I was scared:
the cold shawl of breeze,
and hunched hills; what the water held
of deadheads, ticking nuclear hulls.

Who rowed, and who kept their peace?
Who hauled salt-air and stars
deep into their lungs, were not reassured;
and who first noticed the loch's
phosphorescence, so, like a twittering nest
washed from the rushes, an astonished
small boat of saints, we watched water shine
on our fingers and oars,
the magic dart of our bow wave?

It was surely foolhardy, such a broad loch, a tide,
but we live – and even have children
to women and men we had yet to meet
that night we set out, calling our own
the sky and salt-water, wounded hills
dark-starred by blaeberries, the glimmering anklets
we wore in the shallows
as we shipped oars and jumped,
to draw the boat safe, high at the cottage shore.

The Soldier

They're still clan here, Wilkies and Melvilles;
names painted on plumbers' and joiners' vans
are those carved out, regiment by regiment
under the soldier in his stone kilt.

He still holds his rifle, almost gently,
as you'd touch the uncertain
neck of a dog, his beret still tilted,
pockets stuffed with baccy, letters from home.

Below him, though he'd never know,
four benches face the plinth; but the mothers
favour the play-park sloping under trees
toward the river, with trampolines and swings.

– Benches, and borders laid only last week
by a squad of council gardeners:
two men, a gaffer, and a daft-looking laddie
who pulled up with marigolds trembling in a trailer

while the soldier kept watch. Traffic passed,
Ford Fiestas, bass-beat pounding,
and a tractor, too far to be heard,
turned up and down, baling hay or something,

while below, behind his angle of land,
this summer afternoon, late in the century:
just the old folks' lovely thunk of bowls
a call, applause, a small sufficiency.

W.N. HERBERT

The Pheasant Lesson

Every evening, the Metro stumbling
home from school, I'd disturb
at the same point up
the two mile track to my cottage
the same two deer. They'd leap
my headlights, landing in
the usual storm of darkness
that swept up from Portpatrick
to Dunskey, carrying off my electricity,
my phonecalls, the storm-door from
its hinges, and crashing all these
through the harmonica trees
like pheasants' wings.

Every morning, the Metro grunting
schoolwards, I'd dodge
potholes and pheasants in
equal droves, always in their places
like dull brown starmaps.
The hens cleared off pronto, but
the cocks found it hard to decide
between losing face
and becoming game paste,
and strutted slowly from beneath my wheels.

One day the lane was full
of clean Landrovers, waxy Barbours,
and gun-bright faces staring at
my broke-bumpered, crud-sullied, door-dented,
formerly-white Metro.

I wound the window down
and grinned 'Good morning!'
to a chorus of blanks:
the women's eyes ran for the bushes
and the men's double-barrelled gaze
bore through the burr in my voice.
I thought: get out of their sights.

That night the deer didn't show,
didn't jump, and the woods had been shaved
of a churring noise I only noticed now
it was gone. My mind drove back
to a long thin room
in the Carse of Gowrie, lined
with hooks at shoulder height,
like corridors outside old classrooms.
After a shoot it would be hung
with bleary braces, pheasants slung
like children's raincoats.

And from a T-bar at the end,
hooked through its shanks,
hanging with its head in
a bloody bucket,
would be a deer. It looked
as though it had been caught
in mid-leap, before
it could make the darkness, be
washed through the trees
away where all my phonecalls had
collected, where my lesson for
tomorrow would be forming.

Roadkill

That summer I kept hitting gulls
off the top of my windscreen
like breasting a white-hatted wave
as I sped down the country roads:
herring gulls mainly, and
their brown-speckled young,
bulky birds all, that
looking in my mirror I'd see
drop, vertically, from
an already distant impact point,
and smack upon the tarmac.

Roadkill had been bad that year:
I kept passing smears of pheasant,
well-parted rabbits' ears,
the odd pigmy mammoth, hunched by
the verge, malnourished,
obviously dead, and
various eohippi.

On the road to Buckie one blustery day
when the sun tried bursting out
of hill-big rain-clouds, I saw
a series of creatures, half-squid, half-skate,
pale and lurid in that orangey light,
too battered to identify.

Gradually my small white car began
to alter: a membrane-like look
crept over the bumpers
as of a seabird's foot;
the hint of a pale eye glinted back
from the side mirror.
Once as I drove along
the undulant lane to Lhanbryde,
there was a rippling off the bonnet
as of feathers in a fierce breeze.

After the fifteenth gull
the seats seemed to be covered in shagreen,
a seaweed smell came off the wheel
onto my hands, and
there was an isinglass flash
to the windows.

Obviously, the car, under the impact of
so many souls, had begun to adapt.
I started slipping whitebait in
the petrol tank as a treat,
visiting the coast nightly, until
an angel of the sandstone cliffs by Burghead
told me what to do.

That night, having strewn the back seat
with haddock and tangles, I drove
to the end of Grant Street, that looks
past the Pictish fort to the Firth,
and there asperged the dashboard
with fifteen year-old Ordiequish.
Slipping the car into first I drove,
door open, past the last houses, lighter in my lap.

Just before the drop
I jumped, dropping the flame:
the fire quickly filled the interior
with a flicker of white wings
as the car hit the dark waters.
I watched it tumble and sink
the fifteen feet or so to liberty.

Corbandie*

See thi corbie* oan thi wire
i thi bullyragglan* wund
wi a braichum up* o feathirs roond'iz heid:

syne he pints intil thi blast
lyk a collie oan thi brae
at thi cloods that split lyk sheep aboot'iz neb;

syne he stauchers*, steps, and flauchters*
till he dips his heid an grips:
ut's as near's he gets tae flehan oan thi spot.

But he wullna let ut gae
an be breeshilt* by thi breeze
tho ut gees um coordy-licks* wi aa uts micht,

till thi meenut that he waants tae,
syne thon burd wull spang* thi lift
lyk a fleck o ess* that's fleean up thi lum*.

An sae ut'll be wi you, ma luve,
An thi bairn in yir wame*
i thi hanlawhile* that lichters* you o hur;

fur therr's naebody sall ken
o thi cause that maks hur cry
'Here comes in corbandie' – an be boarn.

corbandie: an argument, some great difficulty that cannot be explained
corbie: a raven
bullyragglan: noisy, abusive wrangling
braichum up: an untidy wrapping up against the weather
stauchers: staggers
flauchters: flutters
breeshilt: rustled, hurried
coordy-licks: blows to incite one to fight
spang: leap elastically
ess: ash
lum: chimney
wame: womb
hanlawhile: short time
lichters: delivers

Grey Thrums*

Lissen til
thi baudrins* purr
hur grey thrums til
thi bairnie-o;
she's weavan thrums
intil a plaid
tae hap* aboot
thi bairnie-o.

She's weavan thrums
o moosewab* fur
an feathers fae
green linties*-o;
she's weavan thrums
fae mawkies' fuds*
an thi doon aff a
yella-yitie*-o.

She's weavan thrums
oot o hur dwaums
o claain doon
a hornie ool*;
she's weavan thrums
oot o hur dwaums
o grallochin*
a cuddie-o.

Sae gin ye dinnae
gang tae sleep
ma pair wee skrauchan*
bairnie-o,
she'll weave hur thrums

grey thrums: purring noise	*mawkies' fuds*: rabbits' tails
baudrins: cat	*yella-yitie*: fieldfare
hap: wrap	*hornie ool*: horned owl
moosewab: cobweb	*grallochin*: eviscerating
green lintie: greenfinch	*skrauchan*: screaming

oot o yir thairms*
an hap thum roon
yir thrapple*-o.

Sae lissen til
thi baudrins purr
hur grey thrums til
thi bairnie-o;
she's weavan thrums
intil a plaid
tae hap aboot
thi barnie-o.

The Ballad of Technofear

'The fossil looked at me and winked.
It's rather fun to be extinct.'
Ogden Nash

'The arteries are cloggin
in motorways and men,
they're deep-fryin floppies
in Silicon Glen,
timor computeris conturbat me.

Soon naebody'll log in
on Scotslit but the profs,
and at the first daimen icker
the thrave'll be flogged off,
timor computeris conturbat me.

Grasp the Internettle
in your ain wee hoose,
and ye'll bide in Bill Gate's kettle
wi a far-frae tim'rous moose,
timor Microsoft conturbat me.

thairms: intestines
thrapple: throat

Burns and Hogg and Gibbon
and sad auld mad McGonagall
will be a data ribbon
on some Apple's lap-Macmonocle.
Timor computeris conturbat me.

And the Athens of the Forth
whose Socrates was Hume
will be relocated
to a cyber-catacomb.
Timor computeris conturbat me.

Dons philosophical
and lecturers on golf
will wax pseudo-topical
on Harris Tweed and Rolf,
post-modernismus conturbat me.

The Auld Alliance means
they'll Derridise their grannies
while central government
replaces them wi jannies
post-modernismus conturbat me.

AI has been found
in a bairn in Achnagash:
just insert potato chips
to avoid computer crash,
timor computeris conturbat me.

While feminists campaign
to disempower the DWAMS,
Wee Bam Bam No-Brain
has jist kicked oot the jams,
timor computeris conturbat me.

With a shit and a click
and a short attention span-ity
the bastard pressed DELETE
on the great works of humanity:
timor computeris conturbat me.'

Notes for 'The Ballad of Technofear'

1   Timor computeris conturbat me' is a corruption of a line from the
    Scottish poet, William Dunbar (c. 1460 – c. 1520). The original line
    was 'Timor mortis conturbat me' – the fear of death troubles me
    greatly. Herbert thinks that computers will bring about the death
    of interest in all literature.

2   'and at the first daimen icker/the thrave'll be flogged off'. This is a
    reference to a line in Robert Burns's poem 'To a Mouse': 'A daimen
    icker in a thrave/'S a sma' request' – an occasional ear of corn from
    twenty-four sheaves is not much to ask (by the mouse). Herbert is
    reversing that idea, saying that if, because of computers taking
    over the world, we let one work of Scottish literature be forgotten,
    they will soon all perish.

3   'Bill Gate's kettle' Bill Gates is the inventor and manufacturer of
    computer software used throughout the world. Herbert is referring
    again to 'To a Mouse', in which the mouse is referred to as a
    'tim'rous beastie'. He is inferring that if you become a slave to the
    'mouse' of the computer, you will also become its victim, cut off
    from all other experiences.

4   'Burns and Hogg and Gibbon/and sad auld mad McGonagall'. The
    first three are distinguished Scottish writers of the past.
    McGonagall is reputed to be the world's worst poet.

5   'And the Athens of the Forth/whose Socrates was Hume'.
    Edinburgh was called 'the Athens of the North' when in the late
    18th century its New Town was built to classical designs. Just as
    Socrates was the outstanding philosopher of ancient Athens, Hume
    was the outstanding 18th-century philosopher of the Edinburgh
    'Enlightenment'.

6   'The Auld Alliance means/they'll Derridise their grannies'. The
    'Auld Alliance' refers to a special relationship said to exist in the
    16th century between Scotland and France. Derrida is a French
    philosopher whose highly detailed analysis of texts (known as
    'deconstruction') Herbert abhors. The 'they'll' and 'them' of this
    verse refers back to the 'Dons philosophical' of the previous verse,
    who use Derrida's methods.

7   'AI has been found/in a bairn in Achnagash'. 'AI means Artificial
    Intelligence. Achnagash is a made-up name suggesting some small
    remote Highland community.

8   'While feminists campaign/to disempower the DWAMs'. DWAMS is
    an acronym used by militant feminists for Dead White Anglo-
    American Males – a reference to the preponderance of male writers
    in the literature of past ages. 'Wee Bam Bam No-Brain' refers back
    to the AI 'bairn in Achnagash' who goes on in the last verse to
    'delete' all the great artistic achievements of the past.

CAROL ANN DUFFY

A Healthy Meal

The gourmet tastes the secret dreams of cows
tossed lightly in garlic. Behind the green door, swish
of oxtails languish on an earthen dish. Here are
wishbones and pinkies; fingerbowls will absolve guilt.

Capped teeth chatter to a kidney or at the breast
of something which once flew. These hearts knew
no love and on their beds of saffron rice they lie
beyond reproach. What is the claret like? Blood.

On table six, the language of tongues is braised
in armagnac. The woman chewing suckling pig
must sleep with her husband later. Leg,
saddle and breast bleat against pure white cloth.

Alter *calf* to *veal* in four attempts. This is
the power of words; knife, tripe, lights, charcuterie.
A fat man orders his *rare* and a fine sweat
bastes his face. There are napkins to wipe the evidence

and sauces to gag the groans of abattoirs. The menu
lists the recent dead in French, from which they order
offal, poultry, fish. Meat flops in the jowls. Belch.
Death moves in the bowels. You are what you eat.

Valentine

Not a red rose or a satin heart.

I give you an onion.
It is a moon wrapped in brown paper.
It promises light
like the careful undressing of love.

Here.
It will blind you with tears
like a lover.
It will make your reflection
a wobbling photo of grief.

I am trying to be truthful.

Not a cute card or a kissogram.

I give you an onion.
Its fierce kiss will stay on your lips,
possessive and faithful
as we are,
for as long as we are.

Take it.
Its platinum loops shrink to a wedding-ring,
if you like.
Lethal.
Its scent will cling to your fingers,
cling to your knife.

Small Female Skull

With some surprise, I balance my small female skull in my
    hands.
What is it like? An ocarina? Blow in its eye.
It cannot cry, holds my breath only as long as I exhale,
mildly alarmed now, into the hole where the nose was,
press my ear to its grin. A vanishing sigh.

For some time, I sit on the lavatory seat with my head
in my hands, appalled. It feels much lighter than I'd thought;
the weight of a deck of cards, a slim volume of verse,
but with something else, as though it could levitate.
    Disturbing.
So why do I kiss it on the brow, my warm lips to its papery
    bone,

and take it to the mirror to ask for a gottle of geer?
I rinse it under the tap, watch dust run away, like sand
from a swimming-cap, then dry it – firstborn – gently
with a towel. I see the scar where I fell for sheer love
down treacherous stairs, and read that shattering day like
    braille.

Love, I murmur to my skull, then louder, other grand
    words,
shouting the hollow nouns in a white-tiled room.
Downstairs they will think I have lost my mind. No. I only
    weep
into these two holes here, or I'm grinning back at the joke,
    this is
a friend of mine. See, I hold her face in trembling, passionate
    hands.

The Grammar of Light

Even barely enough light to find a mouth,
and bless both with a meaningless O, teaches,
spells out. The way a curtain opened at night
lets in neon, or moon, or a car's hasty glance,
and paints for a moment someone you love, pierces.

And so many mornings to learn; some
when the day is wrung from damp, grey skies
and rooms come on for breakfast
in the town you are leaving early. The way
a wasteground weeps glass tears at the end of a street.

Some fluent, showing you how the trees
in the square think in birds, telepathise. The way
the waiter balances light in his hands, the coins
in his pocket silver, and a young bell shines
in its white tower ready to tell.

Even a saucer of rain in a garden at evening
speaks to the eye. Like the little fires
from allotments, undressing in veils of mauve smoke
as you walk home under the muted lamps,
perplexed. The way the shy stars go stuttering on.

And at midnight, a candle next to the wine
slurs its soft wax, flatters. Shadows
circle the table. The way all faces blur
to dreams of themselves held in the eyes.
The flare of another match. The way everything dies.

Mrs Icarus

I'm not the first or the last
to stand on a hillock,
watching the man she married
prove to the world
he's a total, utter, absolute, Grade A pillock.

Mrs Sisyphus

That's him pushing the stone up the hill, the jerk.
I call it a stone – it's nearer the size of a kirk.
When he first started out, it just used to irk,
but now it incenses me, and him, the absolute berk.
I could do something vicious to him with a dirk.

Think of the perks, he says.
What use is a perk, I shriek.
when you haven't the time to pop open a cork
or go for so much as a walk in the park?
He's a dork.
Folk flock from miles around just to gawk.
They think it's a quirk,
a bit of a lark.
A load of old bollocks is nearer the mark.
He might as well bark
at the moon –
that feckin' stone's no sooner up
than it's rolling back
all the way down.
And what does he say?
Mustn't shirk –
keen as a hawk,
lean as a shark
Mustn't shirk!

But I lie alone in the dark,
feeling like Noah's wife did
when he hammered away at the Ark;
like Frau Johann Sebastian Bach.
My voice reduced to a squawk,
my smile to a twisted smirk;
while, up on the deepening murk of the hill,
he is giving one hundred per cent and more to his work.

Away and See

Away and see an ocean suck at a boiled sun
and say to someone things I'd blush even to dream.
Slip off your dress in a high room over the harbour.
Write to me soon.

New fruits sing on the flipside of night in a market
of language, light, a tune from the chapel nearby
stopping you dead, the peach in your palm respiring.
Taste it for me.

Away and see the things that words give a name to, the flight
of syllables, wingspan stretching a noun. Test words
wherever they live; listen and touch, smell, believe.
Spell them with love.

Skedaddle. Somebody chaps at the door at a year's end,
        hopeful.
Away and see who it is. Let in the new, the vivid,
horror and pity, passion, the stranger holding the future.
Ask him his name.

Nothing's the same as anything else. Away and see
for yourself. Walk. Fly. Take a boat till land reappears,
altered forever, ringing its bells, alive. Go on. G'on. Gon.
Away and see.

Circe

I'm fond, nereids and nymphs, unlike some, of the pig,
of the tusker, the snout, the boar and the swine.
One way or another, all pigs have been mine –
under my thumb, the bristling, salty skin of their backs,
in my nostrils here, their yobby, porky colognes.
I'm familiar with hogs and runts, their percussion of oinks
and grunts, their squeals. I've stood with a pail of swill
at dusk, at the creaky gate of the sty,

tasting the sweaty, spicy air, the moon
like a lemon popped in the mouth of the sky.
But I want to begin with a recipe from abroad

which uses the cheek – and the tongue in cheek
at that. Lay two pig's cheeks, with the tongue,
in a dish, and strew it well over with salt
and cloves. Remember the skills of the tongue –
to lick, to lap, to loosen, lubricate, to lie
in the soft pouch of the face – and how each pig's face
was uniquely itself, as many handsome as plain,
the cowardly face, the brave, the comical, noble,
sly or wise, the cruel, the kind, but all of them,
nymphs, with those piggy eyes. Season with mace.

Well-cleaned pig's ears should be blanched, singed, tossed
in a pot, boiled, kept hot, scraped, served, garnished
with thyme. Look at that simmering lug, at that ear,
did it listen, ever, to you, to your prayers and rhymes,
to the chimes of your voice, singing and clear? Mash
the potatoes, nymph, open the beer. Now to the brains,
to the trotters, shoulders, chops, to the sweetmeats slipped
from the slit, bulging, vulnerable bag of the balls.
When the heart of a pig has hardened, dice it small.

Dice it small. I, too, once knelt on this shining shore
watching the tall ships sail from the burning sun
like myths; slipped off my dress to wade,
breast-deep, in the sea, waving and calling;
then plunged, then swam on my back, looking up
as three black ships sighed in the shallow waves.
Of course, I was younger then. And hoping for men. Now,
let us baste that sizzling pig on the spit once again.

ROBIN ROBERTSON

Visiting my Grandfather

In a room as dark as his
you remembered colour, in amongst
brown bakelite, teak,
and felt for furnishing,
the black-out curtains from the war.
I saw the blue cuneiform of the crossword
looming under the magnifier
for my father to finish;
the slow valves of the radio
warming like coals
into English voices;
the rainbow spills, for his pipe,
in a beaker by the hearth.
And the fire, of course, when lit,
full of all the usual pictures:
caves, dragons, life.
But being children
we were out too far to feel the heat,
kicking our legs on the high chairs,
nursing our flat lemonade
and trying not to see our blurred ghosts
in the dresser's unsilvering glass.

Once a year, though, it was summer,
and in the great window
were the white yachts of Stonehaven,
the yellow yachts in the bay.
As if colour TV
had come to Scotland, all afternoon
we watched a testcard

of acid primaries
on wavelengths of green
and a lemony blue.

It was a chill parlour, despite the fire,
but leaving was like opening
the door of a fridge: cold
dumping on your sandalled feet,
your bare legs.
Finding my way back from the kitchen,
arms out in the dark
for the connecting door,
I came against
a womanly thing,
some kind of shawl
or handbag dressed in feathers,
which I felt all over,
putting my hands down below –
till I touched the wetness,
neck and sudden beak,
left it swinging as I ran,
leaving half my life behind
with the hung pheasant
and half in my hands with its blood:
cinnabar, carnelian,
rose madder, rust.

Advent in Co. Fermanagh

Two chemists in one village,
side by side,
ours and theirs;
both specialise in cattle cures.
The greengrocer, meanwhile,
doubles as undertaker;
his potatoes
always hard and white,
beautifully laid out.

The town is bottle-shaped
and dressed for Christmas
in a morse code of coloured lights,
marginal snow
in crescents at the windows,
and on the sill,
in the holly's gloss
of red and starred green,
illuminating angels.

Leaning men on corners watch
the circumspect, the continent,
linking their way to church.
Then the mid-day angelus
opens the doors in the street
like organ stops,
for the pinched and raddled
in their penitential suits
pulling children out of doorways:
strings of hankies from a sleeve.

No one watches the soldiers
walking backwards on patrol:
the cellophane crackle of radios,
the call and answer
as they stroll, each cradling
a weapon like a newborn child.

Stooped under hangovers,
the pasty supplicants
file towards the priest
to say 'Aaah' for atonement,
and shuffle out, cowed,
in a cold sweat,
His Body
tucked behind the teeth.

Doors disclose them,
scribbling down the hill

for rashers and egg
and wheaten bread;
Guinness and Black Bush:
gifts for the back room
with the curtains pulled.

Sunlight glints
like mica schist in granite
on the huddled homes
as the rain comes casting down.

Stone circles of sheep
in the drowned field
watch helicopters come
dreaming over hedges:
horse-flies the size of houses,
great machines
for opening the air,
and shaking it shut.
Leaving an absence, a silence,
and a hatch of light
which discovers a door.
The town drunk emerges
gingerly from the bar,
amazed by the familiar;
patting his pockets,
blinking like Lazarus.

Retreat

In the abandoned house
the chairs are tipped,
the coffee cups thick with spoor;
rolled mattresses shift and sound
as the springs return
to the shape of the sleeper.
I have carried the cold in from outside
so find sticks for the grate
and throw in my diaries,
one by one,
'86 to '74.
The years burn well, the wood roaring;
the fire turns the pages,
reads each book backwards.

Outside, the trees stand like smoke;
the moon declines
behind a scarf of cloud.
I want to go where I am not known,
where there are no signs,
where the snow squeaks like polystyrene
on a discontinued path to the dark
knot of the forest.
I want to go somewhere
to let out this life like warm water
and lie there
clean and cold:
the steady heart's diminuendo,
a bag of pipes' diminishing drone.

The Spanish Dancer

after Rilke

The audience in the cup of her hand,
she is a struck match: sparks,
darting tongues, and then the white flare
of phosphorus and the dance ignites
a charm of fire, uncoiling, spreading fast.

And suddenly she is all flame.

She is brazen: glancing round and shamelessly
setting her hair alight, turning her dress
to a seething inferno, from which she stretches
long white arms, and castanets, like rattlesnakes
woken, startled to their ratcheting and clack.

And just as quick, as if constricted
by the sheath of fire, she gathers it up
and casts it off in one high gesture,
and looks down: it lies there raging on the ground,
shed flame stubbornly alive.
Radiant, chin tilted in salute, she dispatches it
with a steely fusillade of feet:
stamps it, pounds it, stamps it out.

Fireworks

'In the greatness of the flame he gave up the ghost'

Foxe's Book of Martyrs, XI

The poplars are emptied at dusk
like blown matches. A gust frees
and scatters the leaves in their last blaze:
the bronze husks catch and cartwheel
round and down the street to the park
in the smoke of a dark autumn,
from the thin, extinguished trees.

In the small lake, what had once been water
now was seamed with smoke,
marbled and macular,
dim and deep as wax,
with each stick and twig like a spilled wick
in the dulling hollow of the sconce:
metamorphosis in the cancelled pond.

By midnight the ice was dished, percussive,
blue-black under a bone moon.
Skipping stones on its steel deck
gave the sound of thrown springs,
railway lines, or fence-wire, singing.
I had scored a tracery of leaving, a map engraved,
a thrilling in the air.

After the park, the garden,
and the bright litter of the night's display:
a stubble of burnt-out cones and candles,
cold star-shells, burst and charred,
a catherine wheel fused to the bark;
scorched bottles, tapers; smoke, hanging;
the softening box on its bed of ash.

Hands cupped around a match's flame:
the blue twist of smoke. Petrol
is the fifth element: opening
a door in the night I can leave through.
Across the city, a scratch of light
disappears. I hear its stick
clattering in the trees.

KEVIN MacNEIL

Fishing Boats and Ferries

She swayed past the fishing boat towards the ferry. She passed by the old seastairs and, after glancing to her left, turned and flashed a smile at me. A *taibhse** of wind shivered past.

A familiar incense glowed in my heart! Her eyes, her teeth, glittered like a sharp noon frost. Her lips were salmonpink, *gu math Leòdhasach**. Her smile had no charm, but a native confidence, something straightforward, like simple food delicately prepared. She seemed to exude a proud – no, a carefree – simplicity.

I frowned instinctively.

A deep stirring in me said, 'Call her! Pull her towards you!'

My reverie was jolted back, back under the mental horizon, by a loud, asthmatic coughing. Our engines spluttered into life, spun us slowly away from the quay. As our home floated past the ferry, she was leaning on the handrail laughing in the lilt of a greasyhaired student's mock-*Hearach** accent

That night passing Cape Wrath, she appeared in the radar and in the finally opened letter (four years old it said, 'Like Wu Tsao, "You glow like a scented lamp in the strengthening dark." *A ghràidh**, let's buy a shining red boat and sail into the sunlight!') and in the fruit tea and in the tilley lamp, which survived the break-up intact.

taibhse: a ghost, apparition
gu math Leòdhasach: very Lewis-like
Hearach: Harris-like
A ghràidh: darling (vocative)

Snow and Salt

Trudging Princes Street in an unexpected winter
heavy with Ishouldhaves and a Gaelic carrier bag,

I can no more shake you off than
convert the Wall of China into a rollercoaster.

(How noble it is to be a man and thus have influence
over love or weather just as a flea adds

to the gravity of earth and hence the stability of Jupiter.)
Can we bring about a change in love? I believed once

that snow was a chill test, silent, bearable,
like the air in a ship which exiles share.

Yet, in this snowstorm, unending and timeless
as white jazz, as thoughts of a girl filled my eyes

with tears, snowcrystals settled on each of my irises.
Improbable, snow, I should love you! Like a comet, you bring
    us relevance.

I picture you drifting through aeons of starry flakes
passing on (unnoticed, say, as one-sided love is),

later to surface, purer, water that is more
than water, a snow-white comet launched in the night

of our grandfathers' grandfathers, whose purpose drops it
with a blinding fizzle into the brine

of a shining green sea-loch, as though to absorb
the first taste of salt could set in motion

a sea change, an ice age, a thirsting for dilution.

The Bar-Flea

Put a noose on that singer, pour me another
dram – have one yourself – and understand:
it is not the lily-fringed lochans of Lewis,
no nor the brownish black hills of Harris
I consider home.
Rather, it's in those wee small hours
and gestures – that special tin,
that crystal tumbler
overgenerously-f–i–l–l–ed
with whisky – aged, poor,
indifferent! –
when my black mood swings
to green affection
which seems to last until
I lurch back
into the chilling English exile
of Edinburgh: the grey kay-lees
in pubs like this, the smiles thinner
than tourist lies, the austere
gothic homes
brooding like gravestones
so that wherever I go
I am in W. S. Graham's
colossal poem
'like a flea crouched
in the stopped
works of a watch'
– which is really what yon guy
ought to be warbling about
and – what's that? –
you're going to throw him out
if I'll recite MY exile song?
I could, but my throat hurts
and my tongue's dry as rope.
Let's sit and do nothing for one more round.

Young Chinese and Scottish

These bastards I feed.
I serve them sourfaced
from this lair's fiery kitchen,
dish up oodles of rich-crispy-chicken
in an atmosphere thick
with soy, sweat and steam.

Ape-drunk, certain, they'll swagger in,
pie-eyed and slobbering on my thin
silken blouse: '(Hur hur) Hello rare
mah wee China doll, er …
Ah'll havvuh speshl (hur hur) sixty-nine
(hur hur) uhna bedduh speshl flied lice.'

My folks tell tales of dragons, but I have tasted haggis!
See, Buddha-sure, I just hunger for dancing, drinks
and a Scot I adore. How I love to not
taste homesweethome in his plain Scottish food.
I'll serve no more. Take away
the Chinese til I'm half understood.

Am Bogha-frois Briste/The Broken Rainbow

1

Cha tèid falamhachd an adhair na chriomagan
gu bràth. Thèid falamhachd an adhair
na chriomagan air latha fada dòrainneach
air choireigin mar phìos ciùil jazz mar
bhogha-frois a' briseadh an àirde.

The emptiness of the sky shall never crumble. The emptiness of the sky shall crumble some dull day or other like a snippet of jazz, like a rainbow disintegrating.

2

Nuair a bha mi òg
bha mi man tìgeir ach
tha mi nise man cat.
Am faca tu, a laochain,
deilbh Phicasso? Bhiodh e
a' peantadh man Raphael
aig ochd bliadhna dh' aois.
'S co-dhiù, dh' fhàs e ainmeil
a' feuchainn ri dealbhan
a dhèanamh mar ghille òg
beag imcheisteach.

When I was young I was like a tiger but now I am like a cat. Have you seen, my wee hero, paintings by Picasso? He painted like Raphael at eight years of age. Anyway, he grew famous trying to paint like a puzzled infant.

3

A' ghealach os cionn Steòrnabhaigh, ars' na bàird –
mòran nas fhaisg, mòran nas soilleire,
mòran nas cruinne, mòran nas fheàrr.
Seinnidh sinn sin, ma tha. Ma 's fhìor.

The moon above Stornoway, say the bards – much nearer,
much brighter, much rounder, much better.
    We'll sing that, then.
    (Aye right.)

4

Abair thusa sradag dhathail
man pìos bogha-frois gun
chudthrom idir.
Chan eil càil ann a bhith
nad dhealan-dè.

Such a colourful spark, like a piece of rainbow without any
weight. It's nothing at all to be a butterfly.

5

Mo nàbaidh. 'S e tòraidh a th' ann.
Tha stiocair air a chàr: Free Tibet Now.
Cha chaomh leis na prògraman Gàidhlig.
Money for a dead language. They all
speak English anyhow. Tha chuibhle mhòr
a' tionndadh na bhroinn
man spaid shlaodach bhiorach
anns an ùir. Tha rudeigin a' fàs an-sin,
cruaidh, man loidhnichean air aodann
cosnaich, cinnteach, man boma dearg
a' diogadaich ann am manachainn Tibetanach
ann am meadhan a chadail,
agus iom-tharraing do-thuigsinn
a' dol na chriomagan gu slaodadh eadarra.

My neighbour. He's a tory. There's a sticker on his car: Free
Tibet Now. He doesn't like the Gaelic programmes. Money for a
dead language. They all speak English anyhow. The great wheel
turns in his breast as a spade in the dirt. Something grows
there, hard, like the lines on a peasant's face, certain, like a red
bomb ticking in a Tibetan monastery in the middle of his sleep,
an inscrutable gravity crumbling slowly between them.

MEG BATEMAN

An dèidh an Tòrraidh

Tha a' bhantrach na seasamh aig an doras,
a ceann an taic a' bhalla.
Tha gach rud sàmhach.
Tha na h-aoighean air am biathadh
is a' mhòr-chuid air falbh,
am bàgh 's am baile glas glas,
's na bàtaichean-iasgaich a' gabhail a-mach gun fhuaim.
Cluinnidh i còmhradh nam bana-chàirdean sa chidsin
is na bodaich, len dramannan,
a' bruidhinn air beatha dheagh-bheusach.
'Ann an dòigh 's e latha toilicht' a bh' againn,'
tha i ag ràdh, a' coimhead a cuid mhac,
is aogas athar ann an aodann gach fir dhiubh.

Gu h-obann sàthaidh a' ghrian a-mach
bannan liomaid-bhuidhe
thar nan raon de dh'fhochann gruamach,
is sguabar dràgonan ceathach an-àirde
's air falbh thar a' bhàigh,
is mar a thionndaidheas i a-staigh
chithear fhathast mu h-aodann
gaol an fhir mhairbh air an àit'.

After the Funeral

The widow stands at the door
and leans her head against the wall.
All is quiet.
The guests are fed
and mostly gone,
and the sea and the town are grey, grey,
with the fishing boats silently putting out.
She hears the talk of the women in the kitchen
and the old men with their drams
discussing a life well lived.
'It's kind of been a happy day,'
she says, looking at her boys,
each with his something
of his father in his face.

Suddenly the sun stabs out bars
of lemon-yellow light
over the fields of glowering corn,
dragons of mist are whisked up
and away across the bay,
and as she turns back to the house
you can still see in her face
the dead man's love for it all.

'S e mo ghaol a' ghrian san adhar

'S e mo ghaol   a' ghrian san adhar,
blàth dùmhail siristeach   a' bogail fo mheangan,
achaidhean sgeallaig   is achaidhean arbhair,
na fàidhbhilean làidir   a' cumail ceum ris an rathad,
na buin fhèitheach,   a' chairt ghlas-chaoin,
a' ghaoth a' siùdadh   nan duilleagan tana.

Thar nan similear san fheasgar   fead nan gobhlan-gaoithe,
's iad a' ruidhleadh, 's a' teàrnadh,   a' tuiteam dhan doimhne
far an snàmh na cuileagan   am froidhneas fo na craobhan;
sna gàrraidhean sgàthach   a' chòinneach a' boillsgeadh,
na rèilichean còmhdaicht'   le liath-chorcra loinneil
is le iadhshlait òmair,   cùbhraidh tron oidhche.

Is tron oidhche paisgidh mi   an gaol nam làmhan,
gaol cho àlainn   's gun cùm e gach àilleachd,
gaol cho socair   's nach tig an t-eagal dhan phàilliun;
tuilleadh cha chuir   am miann an ruaig orm
le sholas seargaidh,   le agartasan luaineach,
le bheul a' pògadh   am balbhachd uamharr.

Cùl mo ghràidh air a' cluasaig   m' aighear air dùsgadh,
ceann cuimir   air amhaich lùbte,
clàr aodainn   ciùin ùrar;
tha do lethcheann de dh'òr,   d' fhalt de dh'umha,
tha sìoda bàn snìomhte   nad mhala na dhuslach,
is sròl sgaoilte   an slag mìn d' ugain.

Mar ghilead an latha   do chorp rim thaobh-sa,
m' uile shògh is sonas,   sìth is caoimhneas,
mo neart, mo mhisneachd,   mo mhiann faoilteach;
ionmhainn d' anail chagarach,   tàladh dhan t-saoghal,
ionmhainn do ghàirdeanan,   m' acarsaid fhaodail,
ionmhainn gach òirleach dhìot,   mo chuid ri caomhnadh,

            nad uchd thig mi gu tàmh.

My love is the sun in the sky

My love is   the sun in the sky,
thick cherry blossom   bobbing under boughs,
fields of mustard   and fields of corn,
the strong beech trees   keeping pace by the road,
the trunks sinuous,   the bark smooth-grey,
the wind rocking   the soft leaves.

Over the chimneys at evening   the whistle of swifts,
reeling and swooping,   dropping to the depths
where the flies float   in fringes from the trees;
in the shadowy gardens   the moss shining,
the railings covered   with luminous lilac
and amber honeysuckle,   fragrant through the night.

And through the night   I hold love in my arms,
love so lovely   it holds all loveliness,
love so gentle   fear cannot enter its dwelling;
no more will desire   put me to flight
with its withering light,   its restless demands,
its mouth kissing   in dreadful muteness.

My love's head on the pillow   is my joy on waking,
a shapely head   on curving neck,
a calm face   light and fresh;
your cheek is of gold,   your hair of copper,
pale silk is woven   through your brows like dust,
and satin spread out   in your collar-bone's hollow.

Like the brightness of day   your body beside me,
all my ease and bliss,   my peace and tenderness,
my strength, my courage,   my eager desire;
beloved your whispered breathing   that would soothe the
     world,
beloved your embrace,   a harbour chanced on,
beloved every inch of you,   my lot to cherish,

                    in your arms I'll come to rest.

Oran sa Gheamhradh

Chan eil stàth bhith toirt seachad gaol gun iarraidh,
gaol do-sheachnadh a nochdas na iargain

Thar rèidhleanan m' eòlais, madainn air mhadainn,
mar a thig deigh dha na claisean, reothadh dhan asbhuain.

Searbh an ceathach a' sleuchdradh nam bruthach,
goirt sgrìob a' chroinn ag iadhadh nan tulach.

Thig, a shneachd, thig, còmhdaich na slèibhtean,
rag an talamh an cridhe na pèine;

Còmhdaich na sliosan, còmhdaich a' ghiùthsach,
còmhdaich an raineach 's a' bheithe ghlas rùisgte;

Còmhdaich an druim far 'an do ruith an fhalaisg,
còmhdaich na sruthan 's an luachair thana;

Falaich luimead nam mòintichean cuimir,
leig le dearmad tuiteam air sòghalachd cuimhne.

Song in Winter

There is no point giving unwanted love,
inevitable love that appears in its anguish

Over all I know, morning after morning,
as ice comes to ditch, frost to stubble.

Bitter the fog daubing the braes,
raw the plough's furrow scoring the knolls.

Come, snow, come, cover the hills,
numb is the soil at the heart of pain;

Cover the slopes, cover the pinewoods,
cover the bracken and leafless birch-scrub;

Cover the ridge where the heath-fire ran,
cover the streams and dank rush beds;

Hide the bareness of the shapely moors,
let oblivion fall on voluptuous memory.

Dha mo Naoidhean air Ur-bhreith

(le spèis do Chatrìona NicGumaraid)

Bha dùil agam gum biodh tu agam,
nad phasgan geal nam uchd,
ri taobh na mara,
fo na craobhan,
san domhan àrsaidh ùr ...

'S ann tha mi gad shlaodadh
tro John Lewis, Mothercare is Boots,
an tòir air bath dhut, Pampers,
pùdar Johnson, sling is pram;
an aon bhoile a-rithist an-dè:
air sgàth changing mat 's cotan,
is an càr air chall oirnn
sa char-park multi-storey.

Ach san tìde seo de dh'aodannan
a' siubhal nan shopping malls
(fad o shuaimhneas mara is coille),
aig check-out is ciudha
nochdaidh dhutsa
fàilte is bàidh.

Mo naoidhean ùr,
dh'ionnsaich thu gliocas dhomh,
mo naoidhean gaoil,
dh'ionnsaich thu dòchas dhomh,
is tu a' toirt orm
m' earbsa
a chur san linn san tug mi beò thu.

To my New-born Child

(with recognition of Catriona Montgomery)

I thought that I would have you,
a white bundle at my breast,
beside the sea,
under the trees,
in the ancient new world ...

Instead I am lugging you
round John Lewis, Mothercare and Boots
looking for a bath for you, Pampers,
Johnson's Baby Powder, a sling and pram;
the same madness yesterday,
for a changing mat and cotton-wool,
and the car lost
in the multi-storey car-park.

But in this tide of faces
cruising the shopping malls
(far from peace of sea or wood)
at check-out and queue
you are shown
welcome and tenderness.

My newborn child,
you've taught me patience,
my beloved child,
you've taught me hope,
as you force me
to trust in this age
in which I gave you life.

KATE CLANCHY

Men from the Boys

Imagine this man as a lonely boy:
at the biscuit-smelling, sour milk stage,
shirt misbuttoned, strangled tie,
pockets stocked with fists and secrets.

The inky boy in the front row desk,
who writes his name, address, adds
England, Earth, the Universe, concocts
a six month scheme for their general good;

gets dressed in robes to bury voles,
makes the cat a home that goes unused
or tries to help the birds with nests;
gives over spring to crushing flies

to keep a fledgling half alive; and spends
dank winter afternoons spinning
treacle over spoons or making tapes
of private jokes with laughter

added later. This boy writes runes
in milk on library books, and *Out*,
Forbidden on his door. You know
that if you grab him now

you'll hold a bag of kicking bones.
He wants no comfort, mother, home.
He'll work the whole thing out alone.

War Poetry

The class has dropped its books. The janitor's
disturbed some wasps, broomed the nest
straight off the roof. It lies outside, exotic
as a fallen planet, a burst city of the poor;
its newsprint halls, its ashen, tiny rooms
all open to the air. The insects' buzz
is low-key as a smart machine. They group,
regroup, in stacks and coils, advance
and cross like pulsing points on radar screens.

And though the boys have shaven heads
and football strips, and would, they swear,
enlist at once, given half a chance,
march down Owen's darkening lanes
to join the lads and stuff the Boche –
they don't rush out to pike the nest,
or lap the yard with grapeshot faces.
They watch the wasps through glass,
silently, abashed, the way we all watch war.

Pathetic Fallacy

You can't get drenched, however much you wish it.
You could stand all autumn on our corner
stubborn as a lamppost, and watch drains fill
and then spill over, puddles stretch to dimpled floods,
and still not feel the rain run through you,
cooling, cleaning out. Your skin's too tight to let it.

You could wait till all your clothes had shrunk
to sodden sails and both shoes had split and curled
like flowers, your hair slicked down to water-weeds,
till your eyebrows dripped clear stalactites
to tide pools in your eyes, but your heart
would go on pumping the same muddy blood around.

For rain is not relieving, nor new either.
It's our own old wet reused, gone acid,
coming down still muttering its boring song of loss.
It pisses down, it spits, it clings like sweat gone cold,
and when its fingers mock our necks, old hurts,
like blackened rotting leaves, resurface in the drains.

The Flautist

Lord, let the flautist get to Ireland
with faith, combed quiff, cheap flute intact.
Let Ireland stretch wooded arms

to greet him, fold him close in a pub
where men hunch in dark coats. Let their feet
start to twitch to the beat of his boot

on the greased wood boards, let them turn
from their beer to hear a tune (learnt
in the interim from a driver or a hermit) form

from the dance of his black-rimmed nails,
whistle from the gaps in his milk-toothed grin.
Lord, let everyone sing. And later,

flushed, with a fold of fivers in his pocket,
send him down to the sea with a barmaid;
let him taste the salt and the roaring silence.

I met him in the city where he squatted
and busked for the price of a passage to Larne.
He said he was nineteen, Lord, was clearly lying.

Patagonia

I said *perhaps Patagonia*, and pictured
a peninsula, wide enough
for a couple of ladderback chairs
to wobble on at high tide. I thought

of us in breathless cold, facing
a horizon round as a coin, looped
in a cat's cradle strung by gulls
from sea to sun. I planned to wait

till the waves had bored themselves
to sleep, till the last clinging barnacles,
growing worried in the hush, had
paddled off in tiny coracles, till

those restless birds, your actor's hands,
had dropped slack into your lap,
until you'd turned, at last, to me.
When I spoke of Patagonia, I meant

skies all empty aching blue. I meant
years. I meant all of them with you.

Double Take

I imagined that you'd miss me, thought
you'd pace your hardwood floor in odd
worn socks, watch the clock sit stuck,

get late to work, type my name *caps lock*,
press and hold *shift/break*, miss buses, meals,
or sit with fork half-way, lost, for minutes,

hours, sleep badly, late, dream chases, shake,
send fingers out to pad the pillow, find
my hollow, start awake, roll over, hug a gap,

an ache, take a walk, damp dawn, of course,
wrapped in a mac with the collar up, glimpse
a slice of face, tap a stranger's back, draw a blank;

as I have. Each time, I run to press your face
to mine, mine, shining with imagined rain.

Heliograph

(after *Lecture on a Shadow*)

This, my love, if we believe John Donne,
is the best we'll get, love's brief high noon –
       it seems we've just walked out
       blinking, pallid, ill-equipped,
sans sun cream, phrase book, hat
into a marble mezzogiorno square
       after years in a damp cloister.
       We tread the burning ground like cats,
      crush short shadows underfoot –
      I've never been much good with heat.
      I shake, and turn to you, and stick

nuzzling for a scrap of shade. From here
you're statuesque, but bleared –

there's too much sun. Hold me close –
and straight, we're here to pose
       for a photograph, a portrait
       on self-timer. We'll look like tourists,
I expect: crumpled, modern, lost
holding up incongruous thumbs
       under faces shadowed deep as skulls –
       hopelessly small and un-baroque.
      It's hard to smile in direct light.
      Let's shut our eyes, count down the ticks
      and when we open at the click, squint

and see, beyond the square, a gap of shade –
an arch, an opening, a colonnade of days.

ANGELA McSEVENEY

The Freedom

The short-sighted never need modesty
even in a communal changing room.

Bodyless voices din at me
floating over the cubicle curtain
rippling against the wet tiles.

– This swimsuit makes me fat.
– God, look at my stomach.

A bumless fifteen year-old blushes
as she slips a penny
into the weighing machine.

I strip off
confident that I am as blurred
as the bodies around me.

I'm too out of focus
to concentrate on cellulite, wrinkles, pot bellies.

I sashay from the shower room
an exhibitionist displaying cleavage, vaccination scars,
four pale bare limbs.

I who have never sported on a Summer beach
stride to the pool's edge
in turquoise lycra.

Anorexia

I knew she had already died to me
the day I introduced her to my sister.

As understanding dawned she blurted
'You mean she's your age?
I'd have sworn she was forty.'

Insect fragile
she had the air of a stilt walker.
Just a blob of body
on top of two grotesquely jointed legs.

My hopes rose each lunch-hour
but she brought excuses.

– I've already eaten.
– I'm keeping my sandwiches for later.

Or worse still
she might murder a biscuit in front of me
morsel by morsel.

Her eyes guttered.
Features collapsed beneath the insupportable
weight of skin.

One evening she sat at my fireplace
would drink only black coffee
and remarked that she felt the cold.

Even through two layers of clothes
I could make out bands of rib
where her breasts should have been.

Failed dieter in D cups,
dimpled at elbow, belly, thighs,
I gazed at the incarnation of all my dreams.

Unemployed

When the door slams for the fourth time
my hasty goodbye hangs unheard
at the ceiling.

That last pair of feet is running late
to a nine o'clock deadline.

I too rose early.
'How did your day go?' dares me
to have an unrehearsed reply.

I annoy myself by feeling abused
when I agree to wait in for tradesmen.

I eat lunch alone
staring at the draining board.

As I rinse my cup and plate
the unwashed breakfast dishes watch me.

Perhaps mothers feel like this, minimising the mess
with yesterday's cold vegetables.

Night Shift

I would wake up when I heard Dad
coming in at the front door.

The others slept through his early morning noises:
a toilet flush, one cup of tea boiling.

There seemed no place for him
at home all day Saturday
and most of Sunday.

His skin paled
apart from one weather-beaten patch
at his throat:

'It's no life for a man,' he sometimes grumbled
'this living like a mole.'

During school holidays I made
no noise at home.

Mum went to parents' nights alone.
She was sick of darning where industrial acid
ate away his clothes.

At five o'clock I'd be sent
to waken Dad for tea.

The curtains in my parents' room
were almost always closed.

The Pictures

To avoid distracting the workers
the mill windows were set in the roof.

Consequently my mother never saw sense
in spending an evening in the cinema
with no air and not even light.

But she did go to see *Gone With The Wind*
when it first came out.

It was the same day Bessie Henderson's hair
caught in her loom and she was scalped.

The men came running
but they were no use, fainting and going on.

A woman had to hold Bessie up
while an engineer cut her loose.
The worst of it was she didn't faint.

Bessie should have been one of the girls
who went to see *Gone With The Wind*.

My mother tried
but she couldn't like it much.

Ponytail

My old ponytail lies curled in a top drawer
among the usual clutter
of scarves and purses and combs.

It's kept neat in the same plastic bag
that the hairdresser put it in
on that first trip to her salon.

The baptismal snips
grated at the nape of my neck.

She gathered up handfuls
like she was stooking hay
and put it aside for me.

For a few years I could still detect
the medicated scent of dandruff shampoo
but now it smells of polythene.

I take it out from time to time
and I'm always amazed
by how alive it is.

It's never aged or withered or faded.

Far more vivid evidence than family snaps
or formal school portraits
that I once existed aged twelve.

I'm going grey now,
have hints of varicose veins, dropped breasts,
a dodgy back.

But the ponytail is still glossy.
It never lost its colour or bounce,
still has the auburn highlights my mother loved.

ELIZABETH BURNS

Going Back to Chapelton

July, barefoot, she is running outside
for breathfuls of the clean breezy air that ruffles
the sycamore, brushes the fur of the barley
while the valley full of pastel fields
is lit by the passing of pale sun
that drifts through clouds to Dunsinane.

Here at the border between garden and farm
they plant out little cabbages
opal leaves flopping onto black soil
and unearth yellowed pebbles of potatoes
and carrots, wrinkled and minute as babies' fingers.
Witchlike, she slices them in with the peas

startled emerald and sweet from their pods
then there are bowlfuls of scarlet strawberries
unwashed, earthy, rough against the tongue
until teeth bite the slice of pink.
They eat them by the crackle of the applewood fire
summer and winter jarring together

and she is dreaming back to how it was before
snow feet-deep around the cottage
iced air frosting your throat as you breathed
and how that evening they talked and drank
in the close circle of the fire, fed flames
that glanced on flagons of elderflower wine

and so covered by the snow of love were they,
thinking its blanket of beauty and oblivion
would never melt as they held close
to warm flesh and woke entwined
to sun skimming through iced glass,
that they never dreamt of passion's thaw.

Mellowed summer is gentle:
marigolds at the door, a nestling of herbs
rosemary, erica, borage, sage
lupins seeded and raspberries become
plump rows of ripe fruit
where then they were bare canes stalking the snow.

But she wishes not for this slack fecund laziness
of summer months with no needlepoint sharpness
to the light, but remembers and weeps for
the weight and delight of snow
its sheer icing and the stabs at the heart
of stalactite.

Autumn in the Graveyard

In blurry reds and purples (colours of musty hymnbooks)
berries, wet with melted frost, emerge from spiky briars,
spurt out, at a tooth's bite, a sweet blood
to be boiled, fermented, into jam or wine, or simply
taken warm upon the kissed tongue.

Fruits' stalks scratch marble, clamber lichened crosses
stained with seeped juice, and with the faint, glinting
thin as spiders' webs, gold trails, filigrees:
symbols of women, drawings of the moon
that weave fine threads through damp leaves, add gleam
to rampant fruit that shrouds the smudged engravings
and devours the angels made of stone.

Colonizers

The colonizers came
to the island
dis-regarding it
desiring it

They will take the coconut
eat the mangoes
rape the women
reap the date palms

They will plant this land
with sugar-cane
and the people will work it for them
chained

The Carib ones
seeing them come
throw themselves
off the cliffs

rather their bones
be in the salt hands of the sea
than the scarring ones
of the slave-driver

and now none but the sea
mourns them
washing the shores of the island
with waves of grief

The colonizers came
to the island
dis-regarding it
desiring it

They will take the hills and glens
burn the houses
rape the women
trample the crofts

They will populate this land
with sheep
and the people will leave it for them
cleared

The Highland ones
evicted
take themselves
off in ships

driven out
upon the mercy of the sea
and the desolation
of exile

and now none but the sea
mourns them
washing the shores of the island
with waves of grief

Jesus Speaks to the Church at Eastertime

I have plans for you
you snoozer
you drowsy sluggish church

I resurrect myself
am off that cross
knowing what torture is:

your hand's palm (place where
sparrow, flax-flower
wheat-chaff were cupped)

has nails hit through it
cartilage crumbles like biscuit
body gapes, blood crusts

I get my limbs out
of those bloodied ribbons
musky gravecloths

step out past boulder and soldiers
into wet grass
Morning in a garden

Breakfast on a beach
Fingers falter at scabbed skin
touch, touch

I shake you like a mother at dawn
trying to wake a child
who flops like a rag doll

You doze and will not look
at daylight
Your dreams are easier

I resurrect
You eat chocolate eggs
sugary and melting

You mix me in with spring:
hatched birds, daffodils
all gaudy yellow things

never thinking of the southern hemisphere
where it is not spring
never looking at the church at the tip of Africa

It does not need posies, ribbons, baby rabbits
It has tasted crucifixion
real as nails or tear-gas

Its gold and green
are not the colours of primroses
but of freedom, potent

But here you lie in bed, snug and indulged
You do not see there is a day outside
and people living in it

Oh wilted church, what rags of hymns you sing
what mumbled scraps of prayers you speak
on the narrow track to your imagined heaven

Oh gaunt church, gaunt people
so silent and not dancing
not screaming

Ophelia

Still harping on daughters

Always the daughter
her movements round the castle
charted by her father

She has a wide-armed gangly innocence
she is motherless and milky
an innocent in the court
Her flesh is thin as manuscript
her eyes are animal and scared
Ribbons hang from her hair
her skirts are hitched up awkwardly
cling to her gawky legs
make her gauche among armour

Always the daughter

But Hamlet – he –
she licks the ink of his letters
fingers the string of pearls he gave her
that swing between her breasts
– he – but he is ungraspable

He will not talk to her as adult:
he confides in Horatio
walks off, untouchable, to man's talk
He basks in the words of Horatio:
the days are not long enough to listen to his wisdom
He wants it to be just the two of them together
plotting Denmark's future:
no women to distract them

He laughs now at the old love letters
he once wrote her, tosses them in the fire
He wants her gone
His words clang in her head:
Get thee to a nunnery

She is trapped in this tilted castle
and this man who has drawn such promises from her
who has given her gifts of pearls
spits in her eye and slaps her face:
his handmark makes a red flag
across her pale cheek

He will not listen, he will not
listen when she says she loves him,
love big as these pounding waves
that salt the windows
Every word she wrote and spoke was true
but Hamlet will not hear her

Each day she tiptoes on a slippery bank –
one step and she would over-edge from sanity
feeling rocks grown slithery with moss
slide from her grasp as whirlpool water looms

This is not the beautiful floating death by water
She will not have her skirts drawn out around her
billowed along by the current
her hair floating like some golden weed
and a cloak of wildflowers scattered round her

This death by water
will be sticky with mud
Her wet clothes will drag her down
and the stones in her pockets
sink her quickly

She reaches out to Hamlet
through filmy salt-spattered windows –
he drifts through her fingers
she cannot make herself heard –

Madness flows between them like a river
They say that his is faked
They say that hers is real

She gives herself over to flowers
and songs and bitter-scented herbs
rubbed and rubbed through her fingers

It is very hazy and blossomy here, and loud –
she cannot make herself heard
between the rantings of the courtiers

She is walled by this castle, she is liege
Her father's eyes are on her
The ramparts clutch at her –

she looks to shores of Elsinore
and sees the men set sail
for England, and for France

But she will float away
bedraggled down the stream –
water will take her
She has her pockets weighted
and her hair garlanded

She went down singing
so they say

Ophelia
Ophelia
Ophelia –

At Plath's Grave

Smoke-black Heptonstall
tight-lipped and cobbled
drawn nets, closed doors
curt and wind-beaten

She the freak, the poet
buried on this moor-top
where a harsh wind scrapes the sky
cripples the trees

Her grave in a row of slabs
is slashed with the sparse dates
of her life: waste, wastage
and the twists of history
with its bundle of 'ifs'

A heap of gifts on the muddy grass:
cards and rain-smudged notes
fragments of poems
her own and others'

An abundance of flowers:
carnations, freesias
heather, foxgloves
a bunch of rowan berries

Pilgrims still pulled
in squally rain to Heptonstall
where from a churchyard's
damp chrysanthemums
comes the humming of her words

Untitled Love Poem

to give words to what has been and what you are
is in the face of feckless language impossible
words are such skimpy scrawly creatures such
scant indications of immensities and depths
that trying for definition or for poetry
I'm left with slippery abstracts piling up
as far from what I want to say as printed ovals
are from music when it gets out into the air
paltry vocabulary fails me
scratches on a surface mere hieroglyphics
but beyond this in a sturdy wordless
place of glance and touch I will lay out
offerings of vast unwritten gifts

JOHN BURNSIDE

Brother

You were dead in the womb. They had to cut you loose:
like some diver trapped in a wreck
you lay helpless, tethered to death
by the cord. We hated you for that.

The flowers in a jar
by Mother's bed:
narcissi and hazel twigs.
A kind of sign.

I remember the dreams I had about that time:
the milk in my glass transformed to blood
and still I drank it,
thirsting in your place.

You grew beside me steadily,
your mass and volume echoed in my own.
At night you lay against me in a thick
gossamer of cries.

And once I heard your name.
I always thought you had preceded me;
like any aboriginal, you played
hide and seek with souls.

My only magic, sharp and hard
like a bone in my locked throat,
I wanted you to catch me unawares,
to step into my shoes and walk away.

Otherlife

Be quick when you switch on the light
and you'll see the dark
was how my father put it:
                                catch
the otherlife of things
                                before a look
immerses them.
                        Be quick
and you'll see the devil at your back
and he'd grin
                        as he stood in the garden
– cleaning his mower
                                wiping each blade in turn
with a cotton rag
the pulped grass and bright-green liquor
staining his thumbnails
and knuckles.
                        He always seemed
transfigured by the work
glad of his body's warmth
                                and the smell
of aftermath.
He'd smoke behind the shed
                                or dart
for shelter under the eaves
                        the fag-end
cradled in his hand
against the rain:

a man in an old white shirt
                                a pair of jeans
some workboots he'd bought for a job
that was never completed.
                        And later
                                after he died

I buried those clothes in a field above the town
finding a disused lair amongst the stones
that tasted of water
                    then moss
                              then something
sharper
        like a struck match in the grass
or how he once had smelled
                           home from the pit
his body doused in gas
                       and anthracite.

I still remember
                 somewhere in the flesh
asleep and waking
                  how the body looked
that I had made
the empty shirt and jeans
                          the hobnailed boots
and how I sat for hours
                        in that wet den
where something should have changed
                                    as skin and bone
are altered
            and a new life burrows free
– sloughed from a slurry of egg-yolk
                                     or matted leaves
gifted with absence
                    speaking a different tongue –
but all I found in there was mould and spoor
where something had crept away
                               to feed
                                       or die
or all I can tell
                  though for years I have sat up late
and thought of something more
                              some half-seen thing

the pull of the withheld
                              the foreign joy
I tasted that one afternoon
                              and left behind
when I made my way back down the hill
with the known world about me.

Exile's Return

Hard to imagine it, lying intact,
folded into books: identity
to be assumed like tartan,
or spelt out on museum clocks
from heretic stones and peat-blacked pots,
history by strip light. Do we know
where we are in these tourist hills?
Is it plantain we chew to draw the taste
our childhood was? The soft, even names
come easily, we have the voice for them, we know
the stories of threadwork and burning turf
and supple hands that gather in a storm.
And when we reach the narrow, choppy loch
we remember the legends of giant fish
that no one believed and everybody told
as we drove south that morning, years ago,
pretending we could find our own way home.

The Men's Harbour

Late November, Anstruther

The eider are back
                Formal as decoys
they sit at the end of the quay
in the day's first warmth;
Sunday: when the townsmen bring their sons
to fish off the dock,
their rods propped by the wall, the tensed lines
streaming with light;
the boys in hats and scarves and brightly-coloured
anoraks; the men
sober, reflective; wrapped in the quiet of work
that is theirs, for once, and unaccountable

and I can't help but think
there is something they want to pass on:
a knowledge they can't quite voice though it has to do
with the grace that distinguishes strength
from power.
             Beyond the quay,
a crew of gulls is shredding refuse sacks
for morsels of fishbone, choice
oozings of yoghurt or mango.
They half co-operate, half
vie with one another, butting in
for fatter scraps, then fluttering away,
tracking the tarmac with newsprint and crusted grease.

There's nothing elegant in this, no special skill,
nothing save luck and speed and the odd
flutter of threat: a clownish, loud
bravado.
           Further upshore,
the sun finds the white on white
of the caravan park:
blisters of paint and distemper flaking away

from brickwork and metal;
alleys of half-kept garden between the stands;
the scalped grass dusted with frost; a single blackbird
scratching for grubs in the dirt of the island bed.

Someone has set a flag above the dock;
a thin old man in a jerkin and fingerless gloves
mending a hull, his tight lips crammed with nails,
his eyes like shells,
and others here are working on their dreams
of water: men in overalls or coats,
or muddled sweaters, scabbed with paint and rust.
Their hands are dark with oil or coiled in rope;
their bodies subtle, verging on the edge
of weightlessness; no law to hold them here,
no harboured rage.

This is the life they want, their chosen craft,
working with hooks and chains through the sea-water-cold.
Each of them knows what it is
to have been refused,
to feel the silence swelling in their throats
and nothing to be said, lest they admit
how little they care for anything but this,
wanting a life that stays
untraceable.
               Each of them knows
and each of them makes his peace:
the burden of a given name and place
discarded in a moment's self-forgetting.

They're out at the rim of navigable space
and ready for something no one could explain,
a mystery to fathom when it comes
like starlight, or a music in the tide,
or some new vessel, coming in to land,
one cold, bright afternoon: some unknown craft
with snow on the deck, or a phantom of morning lamplight
sealed in the hull's bright paint
like the spirit of tungsten.

Geese

It happens every time.
We wonder about the geese
on our drive to work –
    passing the ferry
or slowing amongst the fields
of water and reeds –

and they come
    out of nowhere
resuming the game they will make
of distance.

It's reassuring then
    to think
that anything could be
so punctual and loud
their voices splashing in the sky
above us
    and the bodies surging on
towards the light.

In school
    we were taught to admire
the homing instinct
    animate and sharp
behind the eyes
ignoring this vast delight
    this useless motion.

I'd think of them gorged on savannah
    or native corn
an African heat laid down
    in the well-oiled feathers
or mingling with salt and berries
    in the blood.

I'd think of tundra
  birchwoods under snow
hectares of lake and ozone
  and the odd
glimmer of random light
amongst the trees

but I couldn't imagine the maps
by which they travelled:
  miles of surface
etched into the brain's
  wet geometry.

I couldn't imagine
  the pull and sway of home
unless it was play they intended:
  that no good reason
of purposed joy.

Round here
  they mostly arrive
in sixes and sevens
dropping to rest for a time
  at the edge of the firth
then moving on

  but once
in the first grey of morning
  travelling north
I saw them in their hundreds:
  one broad
wave of black and white
  the motion
verging on standstill.

I parked the car
  and stepped out
to the rush of it:
a rhythm I had waited years
to feel in the meat of my spine
  and the bones of my face

and a long time after they passed
I could feel it still:
not what my teachers had seen
    that mechanical
flicker of instinct
nothing magnetic
    no skill
and no sense of direction

but homing
    in the purer urgency
of elsewhere
    which is nothing like the mind's
intended space
    but how the flesh belongs.

DILYS ROSE

Oriental Sunset

Behind the backdrop of a hillside
The sky steps out of her daywear
Slips into her shot-silk evening dress.
An entourage of bats whirr and swing
At her hem, like flustered minions
Making sure she looks her best. No need.
She turns heads everywhere she goes.
As always she's immaculate. Since dawn
She's tried on every item in her wardrobe
Matching shades against the colour of her eyes.
How hard she's worked to please. And if
Her slip-shod jaded gallery is still dissatisfied

She'll dim the lights, tune up an orchestra
Of crickets, hang the moon from her sleeve.
What's more, for those who've tired of tricks
There's this: she'll entertain all night.

No Name Woman

All day she feeds the drunken menfolk
On the terrace: between meals they gamble
Quarrel and groom their fighting cocks.
With one eye on her youngest child
(Grubbing in the dirt for bugs)
She stirs the rice, ladles broth
From spoon to bowl, fans back
The ubiquitous flies. Steaming pots
And hot fat spit their hiss at her.
She wears the same rag constantly

A hand-me-down print wrap, the pattern
Washed away, the hem a tatter –
Eats her dinner standing up
Then clears and lays more tables
Cradling plates to hush their clatter.
When only the rats nag for more
She sweeps the dirt floor clean.

Lesson

Not your one minus one or your rule of thumb
Took me in, not abacus, calculus, logs.
I'd had it by heart but still didn't quite
Get it right so you tightened your grip
On my too small too straight chair
Till I'd learnt the square root of my fear
The sum of your anger. Total the times
I subtracted my hands from your snake-tongued stinger;
My fingers remember. That strong arm slam
(You swore it hurt you more than I) had me
Weak at the knees. I mastered deceit,
Filed wits and nails to match playground jeers.
But worse than the hot shame of tears was when
Your ruthless red pen scored up my defeat.
I can't crack your game, can't beat you yet
But I've made a start, burnt my books.

A Beginning

Riddled was the word the doctor used
As if he'd been devoured by woodworm.
She checked herself for being amused
By the comparison: he'd always skirt
The putting up of shelves. His skill
Was steel on steel, he tempered it
Until he snapped. 'A stroke,' he'd said –
His little joke – 'Of fortune. Look at it
Like that.' She promised him she'd try.

She did. Chalked up the years
Since half his stomach was removed –
She'd had a decade to rehearse his end.
Throw out his boots, sell off his tools?
Of course, she must get round to that
But first, she'll learn to wield
A hammer, drive a nail in straight.

Mr Punch, The Ubiquitous Farçeur

Ladies and Gents, I've been about.
Be in no doubt, friends, brass neck
And balls have always ensured me
A round of applause. Straight up,
I've stuck my snout in every tale
And come out winning. Here I am,
Squazzle between my teeth, a hump-back.
A pot-bellied, hook-nozzled dolt.
Cosh in one hand. Codpiece in t'other.
I've trod the boards for centuries.
Baled out Noah, consorted with Solomon.
Even in Eden, Yours Truly upstaged Adam –
　With all the vulgarity I could muster
　Filled Eve in on the nature of vice.

All that's history. Over the years
I've drawn in my belt, contented myself
With humble pie. A simple man –
Hardly the star I was. Yet in seaside
Booths of run-down resorts, there's
Still no show without Punch. But
Holding the baby was never my line.
That wife of mine has it made.
Out on the ran-dan I'll wager. Me –
My hands full of havoc. This infant
Bawls and squirms. A bald beet-red
Wriggler. Give me a dog any day.

Gave it the bottle. Didn't it sick up
Its feed? Shoved a dummy in its gob
It got spat on the floor. I swear
I tried every trick in the book.
Sang it a song, swung it sky high
(Loves it, believe me.) All useless.
The act, I grant, is a fraction hackneyed.
The bit where I knock Judy senseless
And toss the baby into the street
Has been done to death. And these days
My clean break from justice won't wash.
The public is hot for my blood. Why?
Assault and battery's all in good fun.
And always a hit with the kiddies.

Fantasy

In the dark she comes – piecemeal,
Touchpaper eyes to fire your desire
Open mouth a wet red pout
Collarbones and shoulderblades
Her streamlined arrows to a tilted breast
Nipple pressed against an arm
Elbow pinned to a black silk knee.

But all this can be changed,
The parts adjusted or removed
If you so wish. Each item
Holds its own particular allure.
She is designed to re-align
Her curved contours at your request.
She is, in all ways, flexible – so
Re-arrange her bend and stretch.

She's easily dismembered, stored away
Takes up no space at all.
At leisure you can re-assemble
All her interlocking pieces,
Select the size the colour
Perfume texture you require.
She's utterly reliable and
(Most conveniently)
Feels nothing.

Tattoo

He had it done last night:
Behind the blinds of Alf's Art Parlour
He scanned the well-thumbed catalogues
Until he found the apt motif.

On the left bicep TRUE LOVE presides
On the right a bloody, perforated heart
Bruised and dark as a used tea-bag.
Below, a scroll, forget-me-nots,

His girl's name etched in curlicues.
(It's near as you can get to gold
And guaranteed to come up brilliant
When the scabs have healed).

In the bar, his beer mates leer
At local girls and tease. 'The lad's
Gone soft. It's tax-free booze and
Hard cash turn them on these days.'

He'd wanted something durable
Hit on this hand-tooled brand
Knowing its colours would pale
Its sentiments deepen or fade.

Four Canadian Shorts

1. on the grave of a native child

Face down against your mother,
the enduring earth, as if to keep
the world's plague at bay
your bones clutch the dust.

2. a face in the street

Your broad flat silence is
not so much expressionless
as opaque, a bland mask,
a bandage over ancient wounds.

3. culture

Totem poles flank burger bars
in the mall and at the all-night store
on the highway a line of kids
trade beer cans for candy.

4. native art

The gallery, a reproduction longhouse
reeks of pitch, acceptability
and success. Tasteful nostalgia
is up for sale at realistic prices.

DON PATERSON

Heliographer

I thought we were sitting in the sky.
My father decoded the world beneath:
our tenement, the rival football grounds,
the long bridges, slung out across the river.
Then I gave myself a fright
with the lemonade bottle. Clunk –
the glass thread butting my teeth
as I bolted my mouth to the lip.

Naw ... copy me. It's how the grown-ups drink.
Propped in my shaky,
single-handed grip,
I tilted the bottle towards the sun
until it detonated with light,
my lips pursed like a trumpeter's.

11:00: Baldovan

Base Camp. Horizontal sleet. Two small boys
have raised the steel flag of the 20 terminus:

me and Ross Mudie are going up the Hilltown
for the first time ever on our own.

I'm weighing up my spending power: the shillings,
tanners, black pennies, florins with bald kings,

the cold blazonry of a half-crown, threepenny bits
like thick cogs, making them chank together in my pockets.

I plan to buy comics,
sweeties, and magic tricks.

However, I am obscurely worried, as usual,
over matters of procedure, the protocol of travel,

and keep asking Ross the same questions:
where we should sit, when to pull the bell, even

if we have enough money for the fare,
whispering, *Are ye sure? Are ye sure?*

I cannot know the little good it will do me;
the bus will let us down in another country

with the wrong streets and streets that suddenly forget
their names at crossroads or in building-sites

and where no one will have heard of the sweets we ask for
and the man will shake the coins from our fists onto the
    counter

and call for his wife to come through, come through and see
    this
and if we ever make it home again, the bus

will draw into the charred wreck of itself
and we will enter the land at the point we left off

only our voices sound funny and all the houses are gone
and the rain tastes like kelly and black waves fold in

very slowly at the foot of Macalpine Road
and our sisters and mothers are fifty years dead.

Close

She was two months late.
Our tiny ghost
ignored the threats
and blithely crossed

her final deadline,
the sincerity
of its ambition
embarrassing me.

As we stood in file
at the taxi-rank
beside the pool
we watched some drunk

practically choke
trying to demonstrate
the butterfly stroke
to his drunken mate.

Bowing, the swimmer
left his audience
with the prefatory shimmer
of the dream sequence

as briefly, water
rewrote the lines,
shuffling the letters
of the High Street signs.

Too weak to stand,
the muggy night
slumped to the ground
while we both fought

for breathing space:
the acrid drizzle
stung my face
like pins and needles.

The Visit

One night last summer
I was lying in bed, unable to sleep,
the balcony and front door
thrown open to the hot night,
when Death walked into the house.

He swept up to her bedside
without so much as a glance
in my direction, and set about
snapping something very fine
between his long, delicate fingers.

What are you doing? I hissed –
but soundlessly, as though on rails,
he slid backwards through the room again.
My little one frowned but only
in her own dream, and I lay

wondering what the threads were
that he'd broken so carefully.
And as I watched her breast rise and fall
my heart grew strangely heavy,
then heavy again with the knowledge.

Wind-Tunnel

Sometimes, in autumn, the doors between the days
fall open; in any other season
this would be a dangerous mediumship
though now there is just the small exchange of air
as from one room to another. A street
becomes a faint biography: you walk
through a breath of sweetpea, pipesmoke, an old perfume.

But one morning, the voices carry from everywhere:
from the first door and the last, two whistling draughts
zero in with such unholy despatch
you do not scorch the sheets, or wake your wife.

Next to Nothing

The platform clock stuck on the golden section:
ten to three. A frozen sun. The dead
acoustic of a small county; a dog-bark
is a short tear in the sky, above the wood.
The fixed stars crowd below the jagged awning.

Over the tracks, the ghost of the lame porter
stabs a brush along the ground, then vanishes.
The clock puts on a minute, tips the balance

and the stars fall as dust; birdsong thaws in the air.
The recorded voice addresses its own echo.

The Work

My heart was where a hundred dusty roads
crossed and then ran on; or it was a station
full of hopeful travellers, though not one
had either lodgings or a real appointment.
Whatever it was – my heart, within a day,
was scattered on a hundred winds, and sped
through canyons, deserts, river-plains and valleys
to dark ports, sea-lanes, unmapped continents.

But now, like a swarm returning to the hive
at that purple hour when all the crows go hoarse
and sail off to the crags and the black eaves,
my heart turns to its melancholy work
with honey gathered from a hundred flowers
and the hundred sorrows of the gathering dark.

ACTIVITIES

JACKIE KAY

Understanding

1   In 'Whistle Down the Wind' (page 1), 'Dressing Up' (page 2) and 'Divorce' (page 3) we are hearing the voices of children, within different families, complaining about their lot. In each case:

   • What is the complaint?

   • What does it reveal about the complainer?

   • Do you think the complaint will have any effect?

2   Old age, illness and death make special demands on families. Work out fully what these demands amount to in 'Bed' (page 4) and 'He Told Us He Wanted a Black Coffin' (page 5). In each of these poems, what do we learn about the relationship between the parent and daughter/son?

3   Sometimes individuals have to come to terms with conflicts within themselves. In 'I try my absolute best' (page 6), 'Pride' (page 7) and 'False Memory' (page 10), what inner conflicts are the speakers coming to terms with?

4   It is worth remembering that the 'I' of a poem is not necessarily the poet; on the other hand, sometimes the poet is exploring a personal experience. Jackie Kay is a black woman who was adopted at birth by a white couple and brought up in Glasgow. She was later to explore her real parentage. Does that information illuminate 'Pride' (page 7)? How?

Analysis and Evaluation

Mostly, Jackie Kay's poems in this anthology engage our sympathies for her characters by letting them reveal to us their innermost thoughts, feelings, hopes, fears and imaginings. This technique is called 'dramatic monologue'. You should watch for how Jackie Kay changes the structure of the poem, the verse form and other techniques, to suit the particular speaker and situation.

1 In any *two* of the poems, work out with which techniques Jackie Kay seeks our sympathy for the speaker.

2 Each of the speakers has an individual 'voice'. Compare *two* or *three* of the poems to see how the stanza length and form, line length and rhythm, colloquial or formal tone, all contribute to that distinctive 'voice'.

3 Look closely at the titles and endings of the poems. Which endings give us a different slant on the meaning of the title?

4 'Warm, tough, painful and often very funny poems.' This is how another poet, Fleur Adcock, reviewed Jackie Kay's poetry. Contradictory adjectives!
Choose *two* of these adjectives and in a critical essay show in what ways they can be applied to any *one* Jackie Kay poem.

Group Discussion, Individual Presentation and Report Writing

Jackie Kay's poems deal with a wide range of contemporary issues: old age, death, healthy eating, child abuse, AIDS, adoption, transvestism, sibling conflict.

1 In a group, share your personal understanding/experience of *one* of these issues. Has any one of the poems offered fresh insight into the issue?

2 Many of these issues appear regularly in the media because they are of concern to us all. Prepare an individual presentation on current attitudes to any *one* of these issues as found in:

- the statements of national and local government officials
- media reports
- the attitudes of your own family and community.

3 Now develop your presentation into a report which identifies the issue you have chosen, examines the main points of view and reaches a conclusion you are prepared to stand by.

Creative Writing

1 Explore an issue of importance to you using dramatic monologue in the form of poetry or prose. The issue may be one shared with Jackie Kay or one you yourself feel strongly about.

2 Alternatively, you may compose a vigorous poetic response to the speaker of one of Jackie Kay's poems.

KATHLEEN JAMIE

Understanding

1 'The Queen of Sheba' (page 12) is about a clash of cultures: on the one hand Scotland's narrow Presbyterianism, on the other a fairy-tale eastern hedonism (in which a life of pure pleasure is the greatest good). What seems to be the poet's assessment of our culture as seen in this poem?

2 In 'Wee Baby' (page 15) and 'Wee Wifey' (page 16) a young woman is hearing her 'biological clock' ticking. Contrast the two poems: are marriage and motherhood seen as attractive prospects?

3 'Thaw' (page 17) and 'Bairnsang' (page 18) are taken from a longer sequence of poems called 'Ultrasound', about having a baby. In what ways does Kathleen Jamie use references to the garden or to the natural world to explore the experience of having and nursing a baby?

4 'Crossing the Loch' (page 19) and 'The Soldier' (page 20) are reflective poems about the significance of an event back in time: the crossing of a loch at night when the poet was young; the death of soldiers in a forgotten war. In each poem, tease out how Kathleen Jamie goes about recapturing these past events and identifying what they mean to her now.

Analysis and Evaluation

1 In 'The Queen of Sheba' (page 12), how does Kathleen Jamie create for us a sense of exotic extravagance? In what ways is the extravagance heightened by the contrasts with Scottish culture?

2 In 'Wee Baby' (page 15) and 'Wee Wifey' (page 16) the poet adopts different strategies to suggest how her future roles of wife and mother are involuntarily intruding on her everyday thoughts. In the two poems compare her use of:

- the pronouns: 'she' and 'your'; 'I' and 'her'
- the break-up of the lines
- metaphor in 'Wee Baby' and the simile in 'Wee Wifey'
- the silent appearances of Wee Baby and the speech of Wee Wifey.

3 'Thaw' (page 17) and 'Bairnsang' (page 18) are both addressed to the poet's son. In 'Bairnsang' she is talking directly to the baby in her arms, but 'Thaw' could have been written much later, when she had had time to reflect on her experiences. In what ways is this difference apparent in:
- the verse pattern
- the use of punctuation
- the vocabulary
- the use of English and Scots
- repetition?

4 In 'Crossing the Loch' (page 19) and 'The Soldier' (page 20), Kathleen Jamie uses words which principally evoke sight and sound. Compare the two poems to see how in each she switches between sight and sound to intensify her evocation of the scene.

5 Kathleen Jamie is particularly good at creating moods: of reflection, sadness, enjoyment of and need for the natural world, cautious joy.

Choose a poem that depicts one of these moods, and in a critical essay show how the mood is achieved. In your answer you should refer to imagery, verse structure, word choice and rhythm, as well as content.

Group Discussion, Individual Presentation and Persuasive Writing

1 In your group, using 'Queen of Sheba' (page 12) as a starting point, discuss whether the Scots are as narrowly parochial as the poet makes out.

2   Despite her criticisms of Scotland, after extensive travel
    Kathleen Jamie chose to settle back there. In an individual
    presentation or in a persuasive essay, identify why Scotland is
    still worth living in.

Creative Writing

1   'Crossing the Loch' (page 19) is a sensitive recollection of a
    single memorable experience in Kathleen Jamie's life. In prose
    or poetry write about such an experience of your own,
    perhaps, as the poet did, using sight and sound.

2   In a story, poem or short dramatic episode, explore the
    possibilities of a clash of cultures, perhaps one local to your
    own area, or maybe one even more exotic than in 'The Queen
    of Sheba' (page 12).

W.N. HERBERT

Understanding

1 Comparing 'The Pheasant Lesson' (page 21) and 'Roadkill' (page 23), in what different ways does W.N. Herbert show how appalled he is at any kind of killing of a wild animal or bird?

2 In 'Corbandie' (page 25) and 'Grey Thrums' (page 26), compare the methods by which Herbert uses animals to suggest how tender his feelings are for his new-born baby.

3 'The Ballad of Technofear' (page 27) is a tongue-in-cheek attack on the way computers are taking over our lives. 'Timor computeris conturbat me', meaning 'the fear of computers overwhelms me', is a corruption of a refrain from the Scottish poet, William Dunbar, whose fear was death, not computers! What aspects of Scottish life does Herbert imagine will be lost or irretrievably damaged if we are over-run by computers?

Analysis and Evaluation

W.N. Herbert uses a variety of styles and techniques both in Scots and English. He is a poet to be relished for his language, particularly in Scots, where it is worth taking time to savour its satirical effects.

1 In 'The Pheasant Lesson' (page 21) and 'Roadkill' (page 23), what effect does the poet get from carefully, in English rather than Scots, building up the accounts of his and other people's massacres? Do you think that the narrator in 'Roadkill' really destroyed his car? Why does he tell us that he did?

2 In 'Corbandie' (page 25) and 'Grey Thrums' (page 26), Herbert's colloquial rendering of Dundee Scots (e.g. *ut* for it; *thi* for the) gives the poems a convincingly personal voice. These are poems which depend on accurate observation of the crow and cat, but also on a variety of techniques. Work out what use is made of:

- alliteration and assonance
- simile and metaphor
- rhythm and rhyme
- repetition.

3 In 'The Ballad of Technofear' (page 27), W.N. Herbert uses a rich variety of techniques to achieve his satirical effects: juxtaposition of ideas; startling association of ideas; alliteration and assonance; alternating Scots and English; rapid switching between formal and colloquial registers. Find as many examples of these as you can and show how they sharpen the satirical effects.

4 Compare *two* poems by W.N. Herbert, one in Scots, one in English. In a critical essay give a short summary of the two poems and show how the techniques used with the two languages differ.

Group Discussion, Individual Presentation and Persuasive Writing

1 As a group, discuss your own attitudes to the deliberate and accidental killing of wild animals. Do you have a different attitude to the killing of animals in slaughterhouses?

2 W.N. Herbert takes a seemingly critical view of the communication revolution. But is it all bad? In an individual presentation or persuasive essay counter his arguments and convince the audience of its benefits.

Creative Writing

Our tenderest feelings can often be expressed only in poetry. Try writing about someone dear to you, who might be very old rather than very young. You may, if you wish, adopt Herbert's technique of using the animal world to get closer to the human. And you may find that some feelings of this kind can only be expressed in Scots.

CAROL ANN DUFFY

Understanding

1 In 'A Healthy Meal' (page 30) and 'Valentine' (page 31), Carol Ann Duffy reveals the harsh reality behind two experiences we usually feel good about.
   - In 'A Healthy Meal', how does she systematically contrast our normal happy associations with the food she mentions ('tossed lightly in garlic') with the awful truth that it is in fact the flesh of animals?
   - In 'Valentine', in what ways does the poet see an onion as a more real token of love than a 'red rose or a satin heart'?

2 'Small Female Skull' (page 32) and 'The Grammar of Light' (page 33) deal with experiences so delicate and ephemeral that words to describe them often prove elusive.
   - In 'Small Female Skull', how does the poet go about suggesting the fragility of her body?
   - In 'The Grammar of Light', what are the sources of light, and the moods they induce?

3 In 'Away and See' (page 35), the speaker urges us to go forth and live adventurous lives. But in 'Mrs Sisyphus' (page 34) and 'Mrs Icarus' (page 33), each wife has a very mixed attitude to her husband's ambitions. In each poem, what is this ambition and in what way is the wife's attitude 'mixed'?

4 In 'Circe' (page 35) we are listening to a mythical temptress who lured ships on to the rocks and turned the sailors into pigs. What references in the poem remind us about the myth? What do we learn about Circe which is not in the bare facts of the myth?

Analysis and Evaluation

1 In 'A Healthy Meal' (page 30), how is the juxtaposition of food associations with live animals intensified by:

- metaphor
- alliteration
- the use of single-word sentences
- a startling selection of nouns and verbs (e.g. 'swish', 'bleat')
- the punchline effect at the end of each verse?

2 Making us face up to the truth also seems to be the purpose of the speaker in 'Valentine' (page 31). But has the *tone* changed in this poem from that in 'A Healthy Meal'(page 30)? How has that change in tone altered the poet's techniques?

3 Look at the opening lines of 'Small Female Skull' (page 32) and 'The Grammar of Light' (page 33). In each poem the poet is tackling a personal experience but with different tones: one by personal reflection, the other through objective analysis. In what ways are these tones reinforced in the rest of each of the poems.

4 Through dramatic soliloquy, Circe, Mrs Sisyphus and Mrs Icarus betray different attitudes to the men in their lives. Show how the speaking voice brings out the personality and attitudes of the women.

5 Carol Ann Duffy's poems often grab us by the throat in surprise or shock. For a critical essay, choose *one* of her poems which has had this effect on you and demonstrate by detailed reference to content and techniques how she has achieved it.

Group Discussion, Individual Presentation and Reflective Writing

1 'Death moves in the bowels. You are what you eat.'

   As a group, debate the issue of whether the human diet *needs to* or *should* rely on killing animals. You may, if you wish, formalise the debate, with two speakers offering individual presentations at the beginning before the 'floor of the house' joins in.

2 Now individually use what you have heard in the debate to produce a reflective essay. Try to weigh up impartially both sides of the argument before deciding whether it is possible to resolve the issue.

Creative Writing

Reveal your own attitude to love by composing your own 'Valentine'. It can be in the form of a poem, short story or personal reverie. It can be a romantic account of love; but it may also take a more robust, or comic, or even bitter tone. If it is written as poetry, you may care to choose another object to be the key metaphor, rather than an onion.

ROBIN ROBERTSON

Understanding

1 In 'Visiting my Grandfather' (page 37), how does the poet use the colours seen by the child to create the whole life history and lifestyle of his grandfather, and to add to the shock of the ending?

2 In 'Advent in Co. Fermanagh' (page 38), in what ways does the celebration of Christmas not sit well with what is happening in the village?

3 In 'Retreat' (page 41), how do the descriptions of the abandoned house and of the night create the mood in which the poet is so ready to welcome death?

4 In 'Fireworks' (page 42), we know from the quotation at the top that the mood of the poet is not one of cheerful enjoyment of Guy Fawkes night. Work out just how sombre it is by examining the picture he creates in each verse.

5 Identify the phrases and lines in 'The Spanish Dancer' (page 42) which show what is happening at each stage of the dance.

Analysis and Evaluation

1 Robin Robertson now lives in London but was brought up on the north-east coast of Scotland. His use of darkness/light and cold/fire create remarkably vivid visual images. Show in what ways he uses these contrasts:
   - to intensify the child's experience in 'Visiting my Grandfather' (page 37)
   - to suggest the quiet desperation of the speaker in 'Retreat' (page 41).

2 Robin Robertson's dark view of life is sometimes lightened by wit and humour. How far is this true of 'Advent in Co. Fermanagh' (page 38)? (NB To get full value from this task you may need to recall or reread in detail the Bible account of Christ's birth.)

3 Flame and extinguished flame are the dominant images in 'The Spanish Dancer' (page 42) and 'Fireworks' (page 42). Show how they are used to create quite different moods in these poems.

4 Choose *one* poem by Robin Robertson and in a critical essay show how he uses contrasting images of light/darkness and fire/cold to capture his mood and to achieve the special effects of the ending.

Group Discussion, Individual Presentation and Report Writing

1 All over the world one of the main causes of war and social conflict is religious intolerance. As a group, discuss whether, if there were no religions, the world would really be any more peaceful.

2 In an individual presentation, argue that in the western world 'Celebrating Christmas is a contradiction in terms'. Or write a report of your own experience of a recent Christmas, not commenting but instead allowing the facts and description to reveal its good and/or bad aspects.

Creative Writing

Robin Robertson's poetry is valued for the sensuous richness of the way he evokes scene and mood. But in two poems, 'Visiting my Grandfather' (page 37) and 'Retreat' (page 41), he shows us an alternative method: through narrative and scene description. Try using this approach to create a mood or feeling about a recent joyous or sad experience. You can write in either prose or poetry.

KEVIN MacNEIL

Understanding

Born on the Isle of Lewis, Kevin MacNeil belongs to a culture heavily influenced by Gaelic traditions and habits of thought. In tackling his poems we need to open our minds, all the more since MacNeil draws inspiration from a variety of other cultural influences, like Zen Buddhism.

1   The prose-poem 'Fishing Boats and Ferries' (page 44) and 'Snow and Salt' (page 45) are both about the poet's separation from a woman he loves. In each case look for evidence of what she means to him. Identify what brings him back to hard reality and discuss whether he succeeds in getting her loss into perspective.

2   'The Bar-Flea' (page 46) and 'Young Chinese and Scottish' (page 47) are both about being exiled from one's native culture. Their first lines suggest that the two narrators have the same aggressive response to their circumstances. In what ways do their personalities emerge as very different as we read on through the poems?

3   With 'Am Bogha-frois Briste/The Broken Rainbow' (page 48), it takes time to puzzle out the associations and symbolism. There seem to be many anomalies and contradictions: Are parts 1–4 a prelude to understanding part 5? Do they help to get the absurd contradictions of the poet's neighbour into perspective? Or are they assertions of the culture his neighbour is living in but cannot understand?

Analysis and Evaluation

1   'Fishing Boats and Ferries' (page 44) is prose laced with elements of poetry; and 'Snow and Salt' (page 45) is poetry using many of the conventions of prose. In each poem tease out the poetry from the prose and assess their different effects on the poems.

2 'The Bar-Flea' (page 46) character is hardly likely to be the kind of Scot the 'Young Chinese and Scottish' (page 47) girl adores. Show how their very different characters are conveyed not just in what they say but also in:
- line-lengths
- rhythms
- quotations
- colloquial/formal structures
- loosely/tightly-structured sentences.

3 If you understand and read Gaelic, examine the original Gaelic poem 'Am Bogha-frois Briste' (page 48) and explain if you think anything has been lost in the translation.

4 'At the heart of this bold, serious, playful poetry lies a lyricism brave enough to be defiantly tender as it staggers, pained and joyous, through our times.'

Choose one of the poems and in a critical essay show in what way it is both 'pained' and 'joyous' or 'serious' and 'playful'. You should pay attention to content but also to:
- verse-form
- imagery
- word-choice
- formality/informality of language
- tone.

Group Discussion and Reflective Writing

1 We tend to think of Scotland as one nation, one culture. In fact, it is derived from several ethnically separate groups and cultures which still exert a strong influence on ways of life, ways of thinking and feeling.

Start as a group by comparing experiences of encountering such differences. Expand your recollections thereafter into a reflective personal experience essay of encountering and responding to a situation where cultural differences created difficulties for you.

Creative Writing

In 'Fishing Boats and Ferries' (page 44), Kevin MacNeil manages to tell a whole story in about 200 words. There is no introduction, we are plunged into the middle of the story; it is based on a single incident yet it has a beginning, middle and end. And we learn just enough of the personalities to engage our understanding and sympathy.

To the same pattern, try writing your own short story. It might start from a similar title and though it need not be serious ('Posh restaurant and Cairrie-oot'?), it must end in a separation.

MEG BATEMAN

Understanding

Meg Bateman was born in Edinburgh and Gaelic is a language she has learned through study and practice. Nevertheless she regards Gaelic as her poetic language and translates into English afterwards.

1   'An dèidh an Tòrraidh/After the Funeral' (page 50) offers an insight into the life of what is probably a Highland or island community. What do we learn about the community and its setting which made it so precious to the dead man?

2   ''S e mo ghaol a' ghrian san adhar/My love is the sun in the sky' (page 52) and 'Oran sa Gheamhradh/Song in Winter' (page 54) reveal contrasting moods in the story of love. In what ways does Meg Bateman use references to the natural world to help create these moods?

3   In 'Dha mo Naoidhean air Ur-bhreith/To my New-born Child' (page 56), what compensation does the poet find for having to bring up a child in a city? In what sense has the baby taught her patience, hope and trust?

Analysis and Evaluation

1   'An dèidh an Tòrraidh/After the Funeral' (page 50) is a poem in which the two verses are in contrasting moods. What does the poet do to create and then change the mood? How do the last two lines intensify the emotion?

2   ''S e mo ghaol a' ghrian san adhar/My love is the sun in the sky' (page 52) and 'Oran sa Gheamhradh/Song in Winter' (page 54) respectively rejoice in, and mourn the departure of, someone deeply loved. In what ways are these contrasting moods conveyed and intensified by:

- the verse shapes
- sentence structure and punctuation
- the positioning of adjectives in relation to their nouns
- repetition of words and sentence structures
- the final line in each poem?

2 'Dha mo Naoidhean air Ur-bhreith/To my New-born Child' (page 56) reflects changes of mood in the poet brought about by having to bring up her baby in a city.

Trace how the changes of mood are created by:
- the contrast in scene between verses one and two
- the changes in the verse form and sentence structure in all four verses
- the direct address to the baby in verse four
- the use of alliteration and assonance in different verses.

3 It is often difficult to capture an emotion in words: it is too easy to exaggerate or underplay the emotion, sentimentalising or falsifying it.

Look at *one* of the poems again and in a critical essay decide what Meg Bateman does in her choice of content and techniques to get the emotions right.

Group Discussion, Individual Presentation and Reflective Writing

1 As a group, look again at 'Dha mo Naoidhean air Ur-bhreith/ To my New-born Child' (page 56). Discuss any differences of experience you have of urban and rural life. Consider how these different environments could influence the kind of people we turn out to be.

2 An increasing number of people are deciding against parenthood or, like Meg Bateman, do not want to raise children in towns or cities.

Make an individual presentation or write a personal memoir about a single incident which catches the essence of what it is like to be brought up in either an urban or rural area.

Creative Writing

Often when we start to write about our emotions, neither we nor the poets really know exactly what the feeling is; so it is usually impossible to predict what shape the writing will take or how it will end. Meg Bateman deals with these problems by starting with simple statements of fact or observation and letting the emotion emerge as she writes.

Try exploring one of your own emotions in this way, in either prose or poetry.

KATE CLANCHY

Understanding

1 For a time Kate Clanchy was a teacher in London and she has
   an instinctive sympathy for rebellious or macho boys.
   However, she also sees the problems they can create for
   themselves.

   Show in what ways this is true in 'Men from the Boys' (page
   58) and 'War Poetry' (page 59)?

2 Kate Clanchy is very alert to stereotyping. In 'Pathetic Fallacy'
   (page 59) (which means wrongly applying human emotions to
   non-human, often natural, phenomena), in what way does she
   attack our sentimental notion of rain as a refreshing, cleansing
   agent? On the other hand, why does she in 'The Flautist'
   (page 60) deliberately use all the romantic stereotypes about
   Ireland that she can muster?

3 Kate Clanchy expresses very well the intensity of being in love.
   The experiences take different forms: longing for or missing
   the loved one, knowing that it can't last, etc. What three
   different experiences of love is she capturing in 'Patagonia'
   (page 60) , 'Double Take' (page 61) and 'Heliograph' (page
   62)?

Analysis and Evaluation

1 'Men from the Boys' (page 58) and 'War Poetry' (page 59) use
   different techniques to achieve their effects: in 'Men from the
   Boys' a slow accumulation of factual detail; in 'War Poetry' a
   blaze of metaphor and comparison. But show how these
   techniques are exchanged in the last few lines of each poem to
   create powerful endings.

2 In 'Pathetic Fallacy' (page 59), the poet is taking us down to
   earth to realise the hard truth about rain; in 'The Flautist'
   (page 60), she is indulging in wishful thinking. But which
   poem uses mainly colloquial language and which relies on
   metaphor?

3 In 'Patagonia' (page 60), 'Heliograph' (page 62), and 'Double Take' (page 61), find out what the titles refer to, and then for each poem work out in what way the title adds a layer of meaning to the poem; and how the ending and the title are related.

4 Whether they are her pupils, people in the street, or lovers, Kate Clanchy engages intensely with the subjects of her poems, seeking to understand what matters most to them.

In a critical essay, show how this is true in *one* of her poems and which techniques of verse form and structure, imagery and word choice she employs to achieve this engagement.

Group Discussion and Individual Presentation

1 In a poem called 'Underlay' (not included in this anthology), Kate Clanchy sees the coming generation as 'the future, fortunate, children of no war'. But her pupils in 'War Poetry' (page 59) are only too keen to go to war.

In your group, first discuss your own attitudes to going to war and then why it is still so easy to recruit young people into armed conflict.

2 The boy in 'Men from the Boys' (page 58) is determined to 'work the whole thing out' for himself. In an individual presentation, talk about how far you think you can do that and how far and in what ways you may be dependent on others in order to do what you want with your life.

Creative Writing

In 'Men from the Boys' (page 58), Clanchy tries to get under the surface personality of a lonely, difficult boy. Looking back to your primary-school days, can you now, through writing, try to be wiser about people in your class whom you might have misjudged? Concentrate on what you remember about their appearance, behaviour, relationships with teachers and pupils, interests and enthusiasms, before trying to draw conclusions about the kind of people they really were.

ANGELA McSEVENEY

Understanding

1 In 'The Freedom' (page 63) and 'Anorexia' (page 64), Angela McSeveney explores the highly topical and controversial issue of body image. She highlights its impact on psychological well-being from different points of view. Compare and contrast the perceptions, emotions and attitudes contained in the two poems.

2 The poem 'Night Shift' (page 65) reflects on the strains that shift work can put on family life. How does communication between family members suffer under the demands of a gruelling work routine? By contrast, the emptiness of life without a job is the focus of 'Unemployed' (page 65). What kind of day does the speaker have and what feelings surface because of it?

3 The importance hair plays in the construction of female identity is explored directly in 'Ponytail' (page 67) and more indirectly in 'The Pictures' (page 66). Explain the importance of 'My old ponytail' to both mother and daughter. The poet makes a very clear link between her mother's trip to the cinema to see *Gone With The Wind* – a romantic blockbuster of the 1940s – and Bessie Henderson's tragic accident. What insights about being female arise from the connecting of these two events?

Analysis and Evaluation

1 Although 'The Freedom' (page 63) and 'Anorexia' (page 64) explore states of mind and body from different points of view, both poems deploy similar formal and linguistic techniques; for example:
   - two/three line stanzas
   - occasional metaphor
   - the itemising of body parts
   - the interjection of commonly used, weight-related statements – 'God, look at my stomach.'

Compare and contrast the use of these techniques in creating similarity and differences of meaning and emotional impact in the two poems.

2 Both 'Night Shift' (page 65) and 'Unemployed' (page 65) begin with the sound of a door – one opening, the other closing. Describe how the description of sound, or its absence, is used to convey a sense of isolation in these poems.

3 How is the inanimate 'Ponytail' (page 67) given life in the poem; and how does it connect the speaker, through metaphor and metonymy, with the experiences and emotions of her childhood?

4 In 'The Pictures' (page 66), how effective is Angela McSeveney's low-key style in conveying the horror and emotion of a past event?

5 Does poetry need to be full of simile and metaphor in order to make a powerful statement?

Write a critical essay in which you evaluate how effectively Angela McSeveney's poetry, with its direct style and spare use of figurative language, makes an impact on a reader. You should make reference to at least *two* poems in your essay.

Group Discussion, Individual Presentation and Persuasive Writing

1 Broadcasting and journalism often present information on issues related to the stress of being both in and out of work. Can poetry also provide an insight into these complex and controversial areas? In your groups, discuss the extent to which Angela McSeveney's poems have given you a deeper understanding of *one* of these issues.

2 There is a lot of criticism levelled at fashion and media representations of 'ideal' body images and its potential negative effects on young people's self-esteem and subsequent eating habits.

Prepare a short presentation on this subject, either criticising or defending the role of fashion and the media and their influence on young people. Rework your presentation into a piece of persuasive writing which explains and exemplifies your position.

Creative Writing

In 'Ponytail' (page 67), Angela McSeveney uses an object – her lovingly-preserved, childhood ponytail – to evoke a whole range of sensory connections, allowing her to reflect on her early life and relationships and also to consider her life as an adult.

Choose something tangible (it could be an object, a smell, a sound) which connects you with your past. In poetry or prose, explore how the connection works and reflect on what it means to you.

ELIZABETH BURNS

Understanding

1 Poetry often explores the emotional dimensions of relationships through connecting them, on various levels, with the physical world. 'Going Back to Chapelton' (page 68), 'Autumn in the Graveyard' (page 69) and 'Untitled Love Poem' (page 78) work within this tradition. How does the poet use the physical world to help construct her emotional life?

2 The direct address of 'Jesus Speaks to the Church at Eastertime' (page 72) works as a powerful critique of both complacency within the established church, and the 'dumbing down' of Christianity. Who is targeted in this critique and what are they accused of?

In a very different style, Elizabeth Burns recounts the shared experience of victims in 'Colonizers' (page 70). What parallels are made between the two cultures? What do both poems reveal about the relationship between the First and Third Worlds?

3 The poem 'Ophelia' (page 74), in its intertextual references, is closely connected to Shakespeare's play, *Hamlet*. First, find out what the play is about and, in particular, read Act III Scenes i and ii, Act IV Scene v and Act V Scene i where Ophelia, the character in the poem, is featured. Compare and contrast the characters and events in each text, focusing primarily on Ophelia and Hamlet.

4 Sylvia Plath was a poet who, after a troubled marriage to the poet Ted Hughes, committed suicide in 1963 at the age of 30. Plath's writing uncompromisingly forces her readers to examine the links between the woman writer, madness and history, and the same themes run repeatedly in the fiercely contested debates over her life and work. In 'At Plath's Grave' (page 77), Elizabeth Burns describes the visitors to the grave as 'pilgrims'. From your reading of the poem, what clues are there about the visitors' identity, and to what extent are the themes highlighted above being alluded to in the text?

Analysis and Evaluation

1 'Untitled Love Poem' (page 78) bemoans the impossibility of finding language which adequately expresses the poet's feelings for her lover. How does the form of the text, as well as the content, express this? Through a close reading of 'Going Back to Chapelton' (page 68), decide whether Elizabeth Burns is successful in capturing the intense feeling and sensuality of being in love through her use of language. Do the end of this poem, and the end of 'Autumn in the Graveyard' (page 69), introduce a fiercer note? Evaluate how effectively the beauty and ferocity of love are interconnected in both texts.

2 Analyse how the parallel structures, which are a feature of the poem 'Colonizers' (page 70), create a challenge as to how the text should be read and so make us focus more closely on the issue being explored.

3 What impact does Elizabeth Burns' combination of direct address and strong, sensuous images have on your reception of the poem 'Jesus Speaks to the Church at Eastertime' (page 72)?

4 Ophelia is 'trapped in this tilted castle' (page 75).
- Explain how themes and images of entrapment and the difficulty of making one's voice heard operate at different levels within the poem.
- Explain how links can be made between language, form and content of 'Ophelia' (page 74) and 'At Plath's Grave' (page 77)?
- Select particular images from both texts and explore how language is used, in relation to the theme of madness.

5 Sometimes a poem, through its imagery, can make us view the world in a different way. In a critical essay, explain how one of these poems by Elizabeth Burns has had this effect on you.

Group Discussion, Individual Presentation and Report Writing

1 In 'Ophelia' (page 74), by shifting the centre of consciousness to Ophelia – making her the subject of the text rather than Hamlet as in Shakespeare's play – Elizabeth Burns forces readers to examine a woman's position within a patriarchal society. Hamlet, too, can be viewed as a victim of the controlling authority of the older generation.

   In groups, discuss areas of your own experience, whether they relate to male or female issues, that you feel have been shaped or restricted by the attitudes and values of an older generation. You could present your own particular experience and views as a short talk.

2 Suicide is a very difficult topic to confront, but the high rate of suicide among young males in contemporary Scotland means that it cannot be ignored. You could do some research into this area and present a written report that outlines some of the main causes of the high suicide rate among this group in society.

Creative Writing

In the poem 'Colonizers' (page 70), Elizabeth Burns uses a particular structure not only to reinforce the idea that the relationship between oppressors and victims often follows similar patterns, but also to draw attention to a cycle in which victims can become oppressors.

In your own writing, use a similar approach to explore the relationship between bullies and their victims.

JOHN BURNSIDE

Understanding

1 'Brother' (page 79) and 'Otherlife' (page 80) are poems which reflect on the death of someone close from an unusual perspective. Both poems shift between descriptions of the 'known world' and the unknown world which Burnside describes in 'Otherlife' as 'some half-seen thing'.

Start by trying to identify the different ways in which the death of each family member is described. Then decide which descriptions relate to the 'real' world and which evoke another world that the speaker is not fully aware of.

2 In 'Exile's Return' (page 82), John Burnside tries to describe the very difficult concept of national identity. As he says, it's 'Hard to imagine it' (line 1). What things does he refer to in the poem which contribute to the sense of a Scottish identity?

3 'The Men's Harbour' (page 83) is subtitled 'Late November, Anstruther', which sets the poem in a particular place and time. Detail the scene described and decide what kind of male community is presented in the poem.

4 Many poets write about the natural world and John Burnside is no exception. What particular attribute of the birds described in 'Geese' (page 85) does he explore? Explain how the speaker in the poem is connected to the geese at various points in the poem.

Analysis and Evaluation

1 'catch/the otherlife of things' (lines 4–5)

The quote above from 'Otherlife' (page 80) goes some way to describing John Burnside's poetic skill. He defamiliarises our sensory perceptions and so forces a reader to think differently about the familiar. In 'Brother' (page 79) and 'Otherlife', how does John Burnside challenge conventional perceptions about death? How effective is he in generating emotion in the two poems?

2 'Exile's Return' (page 82) is a poem which never mentions the word Scotland yet explores aspects of Scottish identity. How does Burnside create a sense of this identity being deeply embedded in the consciousness of the speaker in the poem? Do you think that the speaker is entirely at ease with this identity?

3 'how the flesh belongs' (page 86)

This last line from 'Geese' (page 85) sums up the idea that it is a poem about belonging and a sense of place. This is also true of 'The Men's Harbour' (page 83). In each poem, what perceptions and emotions are generated about a sense of belonging? What similarities and differences are there between these two thematically linked texts?

4 'Lyrical, tough, often oddly sinister … they can up-end your mood like a drug or a dream.'

How far do you agree with this comment made by a reviewer about John Burnside's poems? In a critical essay, explain how one of his poems made a powerful impact on you.

Group Discussion, Individual Presentation and Reflective Writing

1 There is an ambivalent attitude towards the brother described in Burnside's poem 'Brother' (page 79). One reading of the poem could be that the description of the sibling's 'death' is in fact a metaphor for the very difficult relationship between him and the speaker.

In your group, discuss some of the difficulties that can arise in sibling relationships. Put together a short presentation which outlines what makes for a successful relationship.

2 Now, turn this idea on its head and reflect on whether you are a good brother or sister. Write reflectively on the kind of relationship you have with a brother, sister or another close relative.

Creative Writing

Artists and writers often combine images and words to create something which forces an audience to think about familiar things in a different way. Think about the way the Spanish artist Pablo Picasso used colour and form to explore new ways of looking at the human form. Use language to create a new way of perceiving. Put together a series of images about something familiar to you and try to shape those perceptions into a short poem.

DILYS ROSE

Understanding

1 In 'Oriental Sunset' (page 88) and 'No Name Woman' (page 88), Dilys Rose offers us, from her travels, sketches of two women – one of whom is a metaphor for the sunset! From a detailed comparison of the women, contrast the beauty of nature with the ugliness of the no name woman's lot.

2 In 'Lesson' (page 89) and 'A Beginning' (page 89), how do the two speakers of the poems face up to their difficulties and to the authority figures who misuse their power?

3 'Mr Punch, The Ubiquitous Farçeur' (page 90) lets us hear the voice of a legendary, fictional figure. In what way is he dissatisfied with his life?

4 In 'Fantasy' (page 91) and 'Tattoo' (page 92), Dilys Rose attacks male attitudes to women. In each poem, identify what she dislikes about them and suggest why she leaves the most bitter comment to the end.

5 Show how in 'Four Canadian Shorts' (page 93), Dilys Rose sketches four aspects of the desperate plight of the native Canadian population.

Analysis and Evaluation

1 One of Dilys Rose's most effective techniques is metaphor and extended metaphor. Explain in detail how she deploys this device in 'Oriental Sunset' (page 88), 'Lesson' (page 89) and 'Fantasy' (page 91).

2 Equally effective are the poems where Dilys Rose builds a picture by an accumulation of detail. How far do 'No Name Woman' (page 88) and 'A Beginning' (page 89) depend on this technique?

3 What do you think is gained in 'Lesson' (page 89) and 'Mr Punch, The Ubiquitous Farçeur' (page 90) by using the voice of the character to build the poem?

4 Dilys Rose has an acerbic wit, highlighted in her choice of words, the endings of her poems and her choice of simile and metaphor. In 'Tattoo' (page 92), what is the effect created by:
   - the word 'scabs' (line 12)
   - the last line
   - the simile: 'Bruised and dark as a used tea-bag' (line 7)?

5 It could be said that poetry affects us most when it engages with real issues. In a critical essay, discuss this statement in relation to one or more poems by Dilys Rose featured in this anthology.

Group Discussion, Individual Presentation and Report Writing

1 Taking these poems by Dilys Rose together, we are presented with a sardonic view of men. As a group, discuss how fair it is.

2 The native peoples of Canada and Australia – the Inuit, Ahiamit and Aborigines – are still seeking restoration of land and/or compensation for their losses as a result of colonisation. Integration of these indigenous people with colonisers has been difficult, and can result in them leading degraded lives.

   Use the internet to research the situations of these native peoples and make a persuasive individual presentation or report on one of these groups.

Creative Writing

In recent times, a number of Scottish poets have found it stimulating to speak with the voices of legendary or mythical literary figures. In this anthology, Dilys Rose uses Mr Punch, Elizabeth Burns uses Ophelia, and Carol Ann Duffy goes a stage further by imagining the speaker as the wife of a mythical figure in, for example, 'Mrs Icarus'.

Try your hand at this technique: can you be Dracula, Cruella de Ville or King Kong? Write a monologue in either verse or prose.

DON PATERSON

Understanding

1 'My father decoded the world beneath' (line 2)

What is happening between father and son in 'Heliographer' (page 94)? How is their relationship portrayed?

2 '11:00: Baldovan' (page 94) begins in 'Base Camp' and ends in 'Macalpine Road'. Trace the journey of the speaker in the poem. Where does he go, how long does it take him, and how does the 'journey' shift through space and time, from childhood to adulthood?

3 'Close' (page 96) and 'The Visit' (page 97) both deal in enigmatic and profound ways with the responsibility of parenthood. Identify the two aspects of parenthood being explored and try to explain what the speaker in each poem is coming to terms with.

4 Like John Burnside, Don Paterson captures moments of perception and realisation in his poetry, often through connecting vividly with a sensory experience. In 'Wind-Tunnel' (page 98) and 'Next to Nothing' (page 98), two 'moments' are captured. What is described as happening when, 'in autumn, the doors between the days/fall open' ('Wind-Tunnel', lines 1–2) and when 'The platform clock' is 'stuck on the golden section' ('Next to Nothing', line 1)? Try to itemise all that is perceived in each poem.

5 'The Work' (page 99) is a very complex poem which presents a real challenge to readers. One area of difficulty is relating the title to the content. If the title had the words 'of Art' added to it, what meanings could be constructed from the text? On the other hand, 'My heart' (line 1) is the first thing mentioned in the poem. Ask yourself, 'What kind of work does a heart do?' and try to construct meaning from this point of view.

Analysis and Evaluation

1   A heliograph is a signalling apparatus which reflects sunlight in flashes from a movable mirror. Knowing this, explain how the title of the poem, 'Heliographer' (page 94), relates to the father in stanza one, and the son in stanza two.

2   Time – '11:00' and space – 'Baldovan' (page 94) are foregrounded in the title of this poem and by doing Activity 2 in the Understanding section you will already have traced the speaker's journey through the text. The poem is organised almost entirely as a sequence of couplets. If possible, try to connect like couplet with like in the poem. For example, you could link the couplets which sound like the voice of the speaker when he was a child which connects, 'me and Ross Mudie . . .' (line 3) with 'comics, sweeties and magic tricks' (lines 9-10). Explain what kinds of patterns emerge and why do you think Don Paterson organises the poem in this way? How effective are the last two lines of the poem?

3   Brainstorm as many meanings as you can for the word 'close'. Now relate your various definitions to the poem 'Close' (page 96) and construct as much meaning as you can about the situation described in the poem. What are the feelings of the speaker and how effective is Don Paterson in conveying these feelings?

4   What does Don Paterson achieve by personifying death in 'The Visit' (page 97)? What 'knowledge' is being referred to in the final stanza? How might a reader's personal experience impact on their reading of 'The Visit' and 'Close' (page 96)?

5   'Wind-Tunnel' (page 98) and 'Next to Nothing' (page 98) are characterised by some very striking images. In Activity 4 in the Understanding section you will have made notes of what is described in both these poems. Now analyse Don Paterson's use of metaphor in each. How would you differentiate between the two 'moments' (line 8) described in 'Wind-Tunnel' and how does Paterson create the sense of a shift in time as 'The clock puts on a minute' (line 8) in 'Next to Nothing'?

6 Perhaps the most striking effect of 'The Work' (page 99) is the mood it creates. Is this more important than 'what it means'? Through an analysis of metaphor and simile in the poem, decide what the overall mood of the poem is and consider how mood and meaning interface in the text.

7 'Sometimes it is precisely because poetry is difficult and presents a challenge to a reader that it is enjoyable.'

Explore this statement in relation to one or more of Don Paterson's poems. You should explain in your essay what was difficult about the text, how analysis opened up possibilities of meaning, and what enjoyment you gained from this process of analysis.

Group Discussion, Individual Presentation and Reflective Writing

1 Discuss in groups the responsibilities involved in raising a child. Prioritise your list and be prepared to defend your choice.

2 The UK has a high rate of teenage pregnancies and single-parent families. Prepare a short presentation on some aspect of one of these issues. For example, you could look at the kind of support offered to teenage mothers who want to return to full-time education.

3 'Naw ... copy me. It's how the grown-ups drink.'
('Heliographer', page 94, line 9)

Write reflectively about what you have learned about being an adult from a parent, grandparent, or other relative. You could consider what you have learned about ways of behaving, ways of thinking and relationships with others.

Creative Writing

Think about how Don Paterson uses shifts in space, time and point of view in '11:00: Baldovan' (page 94) to create a vivid recollection of his early first adventure away from home. Try to write in prose or poetry a narrative that looks back and remembers past events from the point of view of the present.

POEMS IN THEMATIC GROUPINGS

Family relationships

Jackie Kay: 'Whistle Down the Wind'; 'Dressing Up'; 'Divorce'; 'Bed'; 'He Told Us He Wanted a Black Coffin'; 'I try my absolute best'; 'Pride'; 'False Memory'

Robin Robertson: 'Visiting my Grandfather'

Meg Bateman: 'An dèidh an Tòrraidh/After the Funeral'

Angela McSeveney: 'Night Shift'

John Burnside: 'Brother'

Don Paterson: 'Heliographer'

Illness and Death

Jackie Kay: 'Bed'; 'He Told Us He Wanted a Black Coffin'

Meg Bateman: 'An dèidh an Tòrraidh/After the Funeral'

Elizabeth Burns: 'At Plath's Grave'

Dilys Rose: 'A Beginning'

Scotland and the Scots

Kathleen Jamie: 'The Queen of Sheba'; 'Bairnsang'

W.N. Herbert: 'The Ballad of Technofear'

Carol Ann Duffy: 'Mrs Sisyphus'

Kevin MacNeil: 'Young Chinese and Scottish'; 'The Bar-Flea'; 'Am Bogha-frois Briste/The Broken Rainbow'

Elizabeth Burns: 'Colonizers'

John Burnside: 'Exile's Return'

Parenthood

Kathleen Jamie: 'Wee Baby'; 'Thaw'; 'Bairnsang'

W.N. Herbert: 'Corbandie'; 'Grey Thrums'

Meg Bateman: 'Dha mo Naoidhean air Ur-bhreith/To my Newborn Child'

Don Paterson: 'Close'; 'The Visit'

Time, Memory and Reflection

Kathleen Jamie: 'Crossing the Loch'; 'The Soldier'

Carol Ann Duffy: 'Small Female Skull'

Robin Robertson: 'Visiting my Grandfather'; 'Retreat'

Angela McSeveney: 'Ponytail'

Elizabeth Burns: 'Going Back to Chapelton'; 'At Plath's Grave'

John Burnside: 'Otherlife'; 'Exile's Return'

Don Paterson: 11:00: Baldovan

People and Nature

W.N. Herbert: 'The Pheasant Lesson'; 'Roadkill'

Robin Robertson: 'Fireworks'

Meg Bateman: 'Oran sa Gheamhradh/Song in Winter'

Kate Clanchy: 'Pathetic Fallacy'

Elizabeth Burns: 'Going Back to Chapelton'; 'Autumn in the Graveyard'

John Burnside: 'Geese'

The Cybernet Age

W.N. Herbert: 'The Ballad of Technofear'

Kate Clanchy: 'Double Take'

Love's Joys and Sorrows

Kevin MacNeil: 'Fishing Boats and Ferries'; 'Snow and Salt'

Meg Bateman: "'S e mo ghaol a' ghrian san adhar/My love is the sun in the sky'; 'Oran sa Gheamhradh/Song in Winter'

Kate Clanchy: 'Patagonia'; 'Double Take'; 'Heliograph'

Elizabeth Burns: 'Going Back to Chapelton'; 'Untitled Love Poem'; 'Ophelia'

Never the Twain: male and female

Carol Ann Duffy: 'Valentine'; 'Mrs Sisyphus'; 'Mrs Icarus'; 'Circe'

Kevin MacNeil: 'Young Chinese and Scottish'

Angela McSeveney: 'Night Shift'

Elizabeth Burns: 'Ophelia'

Dilys Rose: 'No Name Woman'; 'Mr Punch, The Ubiquitous Farçeur'; 'Fantasy'; 'Tattoo'

We Are What We Eat

Jackie Kay: 'I try my absolute best'

Carol Ann Duffy: 'A Healthy Meal'; 'Circe'

Angela McSeveney: 'Anorexia'

Secular and Religious Perceptions of Life

Carol Ann Duffy: 'The Grammar of Light'

Robin Robertson: 'Advent in Co. Fermanagh'

Elizabeth Burns: 'Jesus Speaks to the Church at Eastertime'

John Burnside: 'Otherlife'; 'The Men's Harbour'; 'Geese'

Don Paterson: 'Wind-Tunnel'; 'Next to Nothing'

Hope and Despair

Carol Ann Duffy: 'Mrs Sisyphus'; 'Mrs Icarus'

Robin Robertson: 'Retreat'; 'Fireworks'

Kate Clanchy: 'Men from the Boys'

Angela McSeveney: 'The Freedom'; 'Anorexia'

John Burnside: 'The Men's Harbour'

Dilys Rose: 'A Beginning'

Don Paterson: 'The Work'

Trials and Tribulations of the World

Robin Robertson: 'Advent in Co. Fermanagh'

Kate Clanchy: 'Men from the Boys'; 'War Poetry'; 'The Flautist'

Angela McSeveney: 'Unemployed'; 'The Pictures'

Elizabeth Burns: 'Colonizers'; 'Jesus Speaks to the Church at Eastertime'

Dilys Rose: 'No Name Woman'; 'Four Canadian Shorts'

Celebration of Life

Jackie Kay: 'Dressing Up'

Kathleen Jamie: 'The Queen of Sheba'

Robin Robertson: 'The Spanish Dancer'

Elizabeth Burns: 'Autumn in the Graveyard'

John Burnside: 'Geese'

Growing Up

Jackie Kay: 'Dressing Up'; 'Divorce'

Kate Clanchy: 'Men from the Boys'; 'War Poetry'

Angela McSeveney: 'The Freedom'; 'Anorexia'; 'Night Shift'

Dilys Rose: 'Lesson'

Don Paterson: 'Heliographer'; '11:00: Baldovan'

The Mythic, Historic and Fictional

Kathleen Jamie: 'The Queen of Sheba'

Carol Ann Duffy: 'Mrs Sisyphus'; 'Mrs Icarus'; 'Circe'

Elizabeth Burns: 'Colonizers'; 'Jesus Speaks to the Church at Eastertime'; 'Ophelia'

Dilys Rose: 'Mr Punch, The Ubiquitous Farçeur'

BIOGRAPHICAL AND
BIBLIOGRAPHICAL BACKGROUND

Meg Bateman

was born in Edinburgh in 1959. Studying Gaelic at the University
of Edinburgh and living for a year on South Uist has allowed her
to find her poetic voice in Gaelic though her English translations
are worthy of attention in their own right. From 1991 to 1998
she taught in the Celtic Studies Department at the University of
Aberdeen. She now lectures at Sabhal Mor Ostaig on Skye. The
poems selected in this anthology are drawn from her second
collection *Aotromachd agus dàin eile/Lightness and Other Poems*
(Polygon, 1997). She writes frankly, movingly and often
humorously about the fragility of human relationships, love and
loss, and family life.

Elizabeth Burns

was born in 1957, grew up in Edinburgh and read English at the
University of St Andrews. She has been involved with women's
writing in various ways – through publishing, editing, and writing
workshops, etc. She is particularly interested in the question of an
identity for women working in the mainly male domain of
Scottish poetry. Her poetry reflects this interest in the woman's
perspective. She is also interested in writing about the unseen –
the ways in which people communicate with one another using
methods which are often intuitive, outside the realms of language.
All the poems in this anthology are taken from *Ophelia and Other
Poems* (Polygon, 1991). Currently, she works in bookselling and
publishing in Edinburgh.

John Burnside

was born in Dunfermline in 1955. He was brought up in Corby after leaving Fife as a child. He worked as a risk analyst in the computer industry before concentrating on his writing. He has published seven books of poetry, two novels and – most recently – a collection of stories, *Burning Elvis* (Jonathan Cape, 2000). He has won a number of awards, including the Geoffrey Faber Memorial Prize for *Feast Days* (Martin Secker and Warburg, 1992) in 1994. He won the poetry prize in the Whitbread Book Awards for *The Asylum Dance* (Jonathan Cape), published in 2000. The judges said of *The Asylum Dance*: 'It is a deeply spiritual book while at the same time a very physical one filled with a wide sense of humanity ... Burnside's poems have the rare power to alter one's perception of the world and of language.' Currently, he teaches Creative Writing at the University of St Andrews.

Kate Clanchy

was born in Glasgow in 1965 and educated at the University of Edinburgh and Oxford University. Her first book, *Slattern* (Chatto & Windus), was published in 1996 and won the Forward Poetry Prize for the best first collection of poetry, the Saltire Society's Scottish First Book of the Year Award, a Scottish Autumn Book Award and the New London Writer's Award. In 1997 she gained a Somerset Maugham Award and was shortlisted for the John Llewellyn Rhys Prize. After several years in the East End of London, she moved to Oxford in 1998, continuing to work as a teacher and freelance writer. *Samarkand*, published by Picador in 1999, also won critical acclaim. One reviewer summed up her appeal thus: 'She explores the difficult excitement of the violence, failure and disaster of human energy without condemnation and with a great deal of vivid compassion.'

Carol Ann Duffy

was born in Glasgow in 1955, grew up in Stafford and studied Philosophy at the University of Liverpool. For a time she worked as a freelance writer in London and more recently in Manchester, where she now lectures on poetry at the Manchester Metropolitan

University. She is a Fellow of the Royal Society of Literature and has received an OBE. She has won many awards for her poetry: a Forward Poetry Prize and a Whitbread Prize for *Mean Time* (Anvil, 1993), a Scottish Arts Council award for *Standing Female Nude* (Anvil, 1985), *The Other Country* (Anvil, 1990) and *Mean Time*. For children she has written *Meeting Midnight* (Faber and Faber, 1999) and *Rumpelstiltskin and Other Grimm Tales* (Faber and Faber, 1999). Her most recent best seller is *The World's Wife* (Picador, 1999) in which women of myth, history and fiction (or, more often, the unknown wives of the famous and fabulous) leap into life in poems which one critic said, 'have the pull of the past and the crack of the contemporary'.

W.N. Herbert

was born in Dundee in 1961 and was educated there and in Oxford, where for a time he taught Creative Writing. His writing has been described as 'a weird mix of Desperate Dan, McDiarmid and Dostoyevsky . . . a rare and fantastic voice'. It includes *Sharawaggi* (Polygon, 1990) with Robert Crawford, *Dundee Doldrums* (Galliard, 1991), *Forked Tongue* (Bloodaxe, 1994), *Cabaret McGonagall* (Bloodaxe, 1996) and *The Laurelude* (Bloodaxe, 1998). He writes with enormous vigour in Scots and English, the voice exploding with splenetic force and Celtic extravagance on a variety of cultural (particularly Scottish) targets. In contrast, he can also write with tenderness about, for example, the experience of fatherhood.

Kathleen Jamie

was born in Renfrewshire in 1962, grew up in Midlothian and studied Philosophy at the University of Edinburgh. As early as 1982 she won an Eric Gregory Award and a Scottish Arts Council award for her pamphlet *Black Spiders* (Salamander Press). She spent some years on a trek across the wilder parts of Asia, which inspired her travel book *The Golden Peak* (Virago, 1992) and the poems of *The Autonomous Region* (Picador, 1993). She won a Somerset Maugham Award for *The Queen of Sheba* (Bloodaxe, 1994). *Jizzen* (Picador, 1999) – the title is the old Scots word for childbed – marks another stage of her life which she links to the rebirth of her country. She now lives in Fife.

Jackie Kay

is the multi-award winning writer of three poetry collections which unsentimentally and often humorously explore the joy and pain of human relationships. *The Adoption Papers* (Bloodaxe, 1991) tells the story – her story – of a black girl's adoption by a white couple from Glasgow. It received a Scottish Arts Council award, a Saltire Society's Scottish First Book of the Year Award and a Forward Poetry Prize. She won the Signal Poetry for Children Award for *Two's Company* (Blackie, 1992), her book of poetry for children, and a Somerset Maugham Award for her second adult collection *Other Lovers* (Bloodaxe, 1993). Her third volume of poetry, *Off Colour* (Bloodaxe), was published in 1998 and her first novel, *Trumpet* (Picador, 1998), won the Guardian Fiction Prize. She now lives in London but makes regular appearances in Scotland, including at the Edinburgh Book Festival.

Kevin MacNeil

was born and raised on the Isle of Lewis and educated at the Nicolson Institute in Stornoway, the University of Edinburgh and Sabhal Mor Ostaig on Skye. He is the youngest of the poets in this anthology. His first book, *Love and Zen in the Outer Hebrides* (Canongate, 1998), has contributed to his award of a Scottish Arts Council bursary. As the title suggests, he is interested in bringing together a wide range of cultures, and the poems vary from prose-poems in English to Haiku and longer poems written in English and Gaelic. The Scottish poet Kenneth White said of him: 'If you fancy a mixture of dancing logic, loving grace and cosmopoetic jazz, this guy's got it.'

Angela McSeveney

was born in 1964 and was brought up in Rosshire, Livingston and the Scottish Borders. She began to write poetry when she was fourteen and later went on to study at the University of

Edinburgh. She has been published in *Poems in Other Tongues* (Verse, 1990) and *Dream State* (Polygon, 1994), and has published her own collection, *Coming Out With It* (Polygon, 1992). Liz Lochhead has called her 'a terrific poet'. Sharp, often funny, her poetry deals with work, the human body and relationships. Her honed language has been praised by the Scottish poet Iain Crichton Smith for its 'clear-water shine'. She has worked in various jobs and now lives in Edinburgh.

Don Paterson

was born in 1963 in Dundee. He left school in 1980 to work as a sub-editor for D.C. Thompson, the comic book publisher. Soon after, he began working as a jazz musician and moved to London in 1984 and then Brighton in 1990. In the early 1990s he was writer-in-residence at the University of Dundee. He has published three volumes of poetry: *Nil Nil* (Faber and Faber, 1993) was awarded the Forward Poetry Prize for the best first collection of poetry and was described by a critic as 'one of the best first books of poems I've read for ages'; *God's Gift to Women* (Faber and Faber, 1997) followed to further critical acclaim, winning both the T.S. Eliot Prize for 1997 and the Geoffrey Faber Memorial Prize; in his third collection, *The Eyes* (Faber and Faber, 1999), Paterson uses the work of the Spanish poet Antonio Machado (1875–1939) to create what might be called a spiritual portrait. Currently he works as a musician and editor.

Robin Robertson

was brought up on the north-east coast of Scotland and now works as a publisher in London. The poems in this anthology are from his first collection, *A Painted Field* (Picador, 1997), which was a Book Society Recommendation, won the Saltire Society's Scottish First Book of the Year Award, and was shortlisted for the Forward Poetry Prize for the best first collection of poetry. It was critically acclaimed as 'a first collection of extraordinary quality', 'the quintessence of what the greatest poetry can do', 'a marvellous debut'. It deals with 'the fugitive nature of things: the implacable coupling of desire and sadness, beauty and loss'.

Dilys Rose

was born in Glasgow in 1954. She has travelled widely and spent nine months in western Canada where she took part in various writers' events. She has been a writer of poetry, fiction and drama since 1980 and is probably best known for her works of fiction, which have been widely acclaimed. They include *Our Lady of the Pickpockets* (Secker and Warburg, 1989), *Red Tides* (Secker and Warburg, 1993), *War Dolls* (Hodder, 1998) and *Pest Maiden* (Hodder, 1999). Her poetry collections *Beauty is a Dangerous Thing* (Top Copy Press, 1988) and *Madame Doubtfire's Dilemma* (Chapman, 1989) exploit the monologue and the portrait in a witty and individual way. She was the winner of the first Macallan/Scotland on Sunday Short Story competition in 1991 and has been a Hawthornden Fellow and Robert Louis Stevenson Memorial Award recipient. She lives in Edinburgh with her family.

INDEX OF FIRST LINES